Fixing Broken

By: Joe Brikman

© Copyright 2021 First Edition by Joseph Brikman - All rights reserved.
© Copyright 2022 Second Edition by Joseph Brikman - All rights reserved.

It is not legal to reproduce, duplicate, or transmit any part of this document in either electronic means or printed format without explicit written permission granted by Owner.

Electronic or Voice Recording of this publication is strictly prohibited.

"The master in the art of living makes little distinction between his work and his play, his labor and his leisure, his mind and his body, his information and his recreation, his love and his religion. He hardly knows which is which. He simply pursues his vision of excellence at whatever he does, leaving others to decide whether he is working or playing. To him, he's always doing both."

— **James A. Michener**

Dear Reader,

  I encourage you to approach this book with an open mind.

When writing this book I did my best to give as much context as I felt necessary to bring out the lessons at the end.

This book in no way is intended to point fingers, gaslight, or single out any one individual.

After reading this book, if you have any questions or would like to connect with me you can do so by sending an email to:

Joe@Fixingbrokenthebook.com

Thank you for your support!

Joe Brikman

I am excited for you to read my book!

This book isn't a self-help book, nor is it some guru pitch for a monthly subscribers program.

This book is NOT the problem fixer nor does it provide a magical solution to all the problems you've faced, and the problems you created.

This book is not a platform to whine and bitch about the lot I ended up with or the hardships I've experienced.

This book is a testament to growth.
This book is a beacon of light.
This book is proof that if I can do it frankly, anyone can.

This book is a collection of my personal experiences and the lessons I've learned from them over the last ten years while growing up and becoming the person I've always dreamed I'll be.

My hope when you're done reading this book is to come out wiser, happier, and more enthusiastic about tackling life's problems. I hope to validate all of the people who feel like they are alone in their struggles and offer direction to those that are looking for it.

I've also added a framework that I follow every day to keep myself organized and in momentum. Reading this book there are times when I feel like maybe I should omit parts of it or not talk about certain things because of what people might say or feel.

I've decided to talk about the things that directly affected me and my life not because I am pointing fingers or pinning blame on anyone for what happened, but because it's important to me that anyone who might end up in the same or similar situations receive the assurance, validation, and guidance I so desperately could have used which would have saved me a lot of pain and heartache.

As I started talking more about my story lots of people have come forward and reached out to me. Sharing with me how they too went through similar experiences and asked me for advice on how I overcame certain things, Yes, It's ugly to talk about and is definitely not the purpose of this book - these details are merely for context about what this was all about.

My goal with this book is to impact society in a major way and change the world for the better.
If you are perseverant enough and push your limits, no one can ever stop you.
Our Success is there for the taking.

For ease of navigation and for practical application, I've divided this book into four sections.

Each one of these sections is in chronological order.

How I discovered them, and how to use these tools properly.

Part one:

How to Train your mind And Own your Future

I share how I went from using my mind as a tool to destroy myself to shifting my perspective and taking advantage of my Trauma to use it for my benefit.

Part two:

Personal accountability and self-control.

We are all guilty of bullshitting ourselves every now and then as to <u>where</u> we are really holding.

This part sets the record straight and gives useful insights to overcoming daily challenges.

Part three:

<u>Money matters</u>

I've dedicated 40 pages of this book to explain modern-day finances to anyone who still isn't clear how they work.
These are things I learned the hard way, and wish someone had told me before I was on the brink of bankruptcy.

Part four:

<u>Building your dream life</u>

I share my **framework for owning your shit,** and discipline I learned while in the Paratroopers Brigade of the IDF.

In these next 352 pages, I am going to share some of the most meaningful experiences of my last 10 years in personal development.

How I Learned to take every situation I found myself in and Repurpose it for what I needed it to be in the moment.

Lots of people I know struggle with keeping themselves in momentum with all of the noise going on in our day-to-day life.

We've all been there.

Chances are if you are reading this book it's because you feel some sort of connection or personal understanding of what it means to struggle, while aboard this journey called life.

This book is an overview of my life from the ages 9-23 as I went from a broken child to a happy Adult.
- I've lived through sexual abuse.
- I was subjected to verbal abuse,
- I've had suicidal thoughts,
- I've attempted suicide.
- I had flashbacks of being raped.
- I lived through almost six months of homelessness.
- I struggled with Alcoholism.
- I was addicted to pornography.
- I self-isolated from my family and loved ones.

My journey has forced me to deal with depression, overcome panic attacks, and pay the price for my own self deprecating actions. I used to struggle with the feeling of not belonging.

Living life for so long in a victim mentality trained my brain to always be complaining instead of always looking for ways to push forward.

This book documents the steps I took to work my way up to where I wanted to be and what I've used to maximize my output and performance.

This book is not for the faint-hearted.

This book is not for you if you don't like being called out on your shit.

This book is not for you if you have an aversion to confronting the truth and seeing reality for what it is.

The point of this book is not to spew random regurgitated bullshit you can find on the internet for me to look smart.

The purpose of this book is not to recruit you for an MLM or any other sort.

The purpose of this book is not to give you more reasons to feed your self deprecating thoughts or wallow in self-pity.

Rather this book is a clear roadmap of sorts that will explain the processes I used to develop myself, in a very candid fashion, as if we were having a conversation.

The views I share here may or may not be mutually exclusive and are not directed at anyone, or a specific individual.

Nor is it my intention to gaslight or shit on other people's opinions, ideas or versions of beliefs.

This is me.

Raw and unapologetic.

Part One:

How to Train Your Mind And Own Your Future

The day I learned how to master my thoughts and will my life into reality, is the day I was given a new lease on life.

I truly believe that I can do anything I set my mind to when I put the work in.

All of the work.

Chapter 1

The triangle of doom is an ominous title I use to describe the vice that a negative outlook, perspective, and mindset can affect your ability to keep advancing towards the goals and dreams you've made for yourself.

It's a simple Equation.

When you aren't clear on what you want to achieve you can't be dead focused on an end goal because it doesn't exist.

When you aren't dead focused on a goal, you end up bouncing around to different versions of the same thing so instead of moving forward and growing you are just wasting energy going in circles.

When you aren't using your Energy properly and go in circles the end result is that you give up on your vision and your goals because your enthusiasm fades and you no longer choose to continue.

Which is when all of the problems start.

For me It looked something like This:

December 2014 found me living on a beach on ocean drive in Miami Beach Florida.

I had picked up and left The Yeshivah school I was learning at in Montreal.

Early one morning I got on a one-way flight to Miami that I had booked just three days before.

The $1000 credit card I had gotten approved for three weeks ago had come in the mail, and I was ready for a change.

I had been battling a lot of inner struggles for almost half of my life already, and I couldn't take it any longer.

I had tried to commit suicide a few years before this, and if there was anything I really wanted to avoid was going back to the same mental dark space that led up to that night that determined my future.

The birthday I tried to end my life.

I used the little I knew about credit, and the cash I had saved up while working odd jobs.

Things like selling electronics on craigslist, selling things on eBay, selling food in school.

Eventually, I sat there one night and devised a plan to break out of the system and never come back.

I was done with this shit forever.

One cold morning at about 3:30 AM my best friend S, watched in disbelief as I got into the red car that was my taxi and headed to the airport.

On to create a new life in a place I had never been to on my own before.

I had no idea what type of rude awakening I was in for as soon as I got to Miami.

My plan until now was to get to the airport, get one of those group van Taxi Things, and head on down to Miami Beach - where the rental apartment I had booked online was. Overlooking the ocean.

I got out of the van and took my suitcase.
I was going to get settled into my apartment and then head out and walk around the area.

This was the first time I was in Miami alone.
Actually, this was the first time I had ever traveled on my own that there wasn't anyone wanting updates as to my whereabouts.
It felt strange but it also gave me a sense of thrill.

Like I was on my own personal vacation.
Finally In charge of myself and my life.
I was going to do everything they said I couldn't.
I was going to show them!

All of these thoughts came crashing down in shambles because when I got inside I was faced with a harsh reality.

The address of the guy that I was talking to when I booked the reservation did not exist.
The Money I put down on this website to book a nice room for a month overlooking the water became history and I was in shock.

I had no idea what to do.
And I had nobody to turn to.

I tried to call the company but they couldn't help me.
I had no plan as to what I would do when I got here other than to get to this apartment and figure my shit out.

The system wasn't as advanced as it is today and there wasn't any immediate solution in sight.

Airbnb said it would take at least a few days for them to look into it and resolve the situation but meanwhile, it was getting late and I had nowhere to put my stuff.

I walked around the building again and again in a trance. Desperately looking for the apartment number that I had in my email and lo and behold it never existed.
There wasn't even a place for it in the bell or a mailbox with the number on it.

I did not know this at the time but fake vacation listings in Popular tourist cities are something that's very popular.
Looking back now I laugh at how naive I was.

It was too easy.

I was too stuck in my own world to really even do my due diligence of vetting the place first and was so focused on finding a way out I got tunnel vision.

This guy had said yes to every request of mine but he also kept telling me my payment was needed right away to secure the spot since it's a very busy season and was very responsive via email and Whatsapp when I spoke to him.

Until I sent payment.

I was very eager to book this apartment for two reasons:

1) I didn't know anything about how rentals worked at all and someone offering to make it easier for me in a way where I just had to pay and show up was the dream way to get out and start a new life.

2) Every movie I had watched that had Miami Beach in it had cool cars and guns and drugs in it which to me seemed like the good life and happiness. I really wanted that as soon as I would have the chance.

There was that one scene I would always rewatch in the movie Bad Boys 2.
Money, Girls, and Nightclubs.
I did not know anything about what it meant to lead a life - real life- other than that which I had been brought up with.

I was a good Jewish boy.

A Chabad Lubavitch orthodox yeshiva boy.

Chapter 2

My entire life growing up was spent in the Brooklyn ultra-orthodox Hassidic Neighborhood of Crown heights. It was a bubble of ideals parents tried to raise their kids on.

The yeshivah system in general and the Chabad education system in particular, as well as its community, are very insulated.

When I go back there I make sure to wear a "yarmulke" (skullcap) and not play any loud music. I can't walk in the street with a friend who doesn't keep Shabbat or who smokes a joint every now and then to take the edge off.

People talk about these things, and if god forbid my teachers found out, I'd be in for a talking to.

It is also a community that did not provide any education about abuse and sexual abuse in particular to parents, teachers, and community members, nor did it help with when a concern was brought up about someone being an abuser or sexual offender: these claims fell on semi deaf ears, and were swept under the rug.

To this day I feel a lot of cases are still not addressed properly.

Growing up, I was harmed by this.

Even while I was still living at home, and going to school, I felt like I was left to fend for myself.

Trying to lead any sort of normal life while being a teenager is tough.

Trying to lead a normal life while being a victim of severe childhood sexual abuse and rape is excruciating.

I did not have any sort of education to know and understand the symptoms or, what had happened to me, I was so young, that for a long time I didn't even know there was a context for what had taken place.

Abuse in religious communities is a hard topic and the Hassidic community is no different.

I found it all very ironic.

My whole life growing up I was told the internet was bad, and that everyone other than us - the "Chosen" Jewish people were Goyim - other nations - which were evil people always trying to harm us.

While **at the very same time** the teachers themselves would molest kids in school and the community really wasn't doing anything to stop it.

Whether they knew what was going on or not, there was a certain pattern of behaviors by different people (Teachers, educators, community leaders) that went swept under the rug, and day by day, more and more people were getting affected.

For me, it happened when I was just a boy, not even ten years old.

My abuser though wasn't a rabbi.
My abuser was my Babysitter.

I don't remember exactly what day of the month it was or even what day of the week it all started, but I do remember my mother not being home and my father being out of town for a conference.

There was this babysitter we had who used to take care of us after we'd come home from school, and when things got busy she would come over to our house as well and watch us while my mom was at school, and my dad was at work.

She always was very nice and delicate when she was in the presence of my parents and others, but in my house, she was the devil woman.

One day it just kind of happened.

She was angry at something and bent me over and started slapping my butt.
She took my pants down and began spanking me.
She took me in her arms and stripped me naked.
After me alarmingly asking her to stop she bent me over, and put both her hands on my buttocks, spreading them apart.

She took one of her fingers and inserted it into my body.
She raped me.
She looked me in the eyes with a devil glare of pleasure as blood trickled down my leg.

I let out a small sob as tears trickled down my cheeks. First one, then another, then I was trembling uncontrollably, my body shaking with fear and pain.

What the actual fuck had just happened?!

She stopped hurting me and gave me a hug.

Comforting me until I calmed down.
The whole idea of it was sick.

She hurt me and then calmed me down and comforted me.
All the while reminding me that I mustn't share anything that had transpired with anyone lest she finds out.

From then on it was Every chance she had with me alone.

She'd offer to take me out for ice cream and buy me gifts which although might have seemed a little strange to my parents - she was an older single woman who had a very close connection to us because of all the time she worked with us. I guess It sort of made sense?

What is a kid supposed to do when he is physically violated but he has no idea what transpired?

I for one felt a very deep shame.

I did not know what sex meant, nor did I have any understanding as to what had actually happened. Something between the way she always threatened me if I told anyone what had happened, and made sure I understood what she meant when she said she'd hurt me if I told anyone, not that I really understood what she meant but I had the living fear of God struck in me from telling a soul.

When I got about the age of 11 and hit puberty, I did not yet understand what exactly had happened to me but I kept having flashbacks and felt like I had no one to talk to and explain how I felt.

Not that I had the words to explain those feelings anyway.

I fell into a very deep depression.

Chapter 3

When I was about the same age, I moved out from sharing a room with my younger brother into my own room in our basement, after convincing my parents I was capable of having my own room.

The basement had its own door off the back of the kitchen, and it had access to the side door.

The first thing I did, being that I was now alone, was to get a device that had internet capability.

An iPod touch.

This was the first thing I was anxious to do, was to start learning more about what had happened to me.

I had so many questions I needed answers to.

Getting the phone in its own right was a major feat.

I had to covertly take extra snacks from home to sell to kids at school to make a few bucks.

Once I did that, I started going to this one corner store that sold A soda called Tropical fantasy and Wise potato Chips (which most of my friends weren't allowed to eat at home because they were not considered kosher enough) and brought them to school to sell to the kids in my class.

I had been selling things for as long as I can remember. From the day I learned that money was a commodity that people exchange for shit they want to have, I understood that I'd have to get some.

My father also owned a retail store in the community and from a very early age, I saw that hard work was rewarded.

As I grew up I learned that money is a yardstick to measure the level of service you provide to your customers.

The better your service is, the more valuable you are.

My father personified that.

He was a brilliant businessman.
 He was everything I could have asked for in a dad.

I have fond memories of him growing up.

He was funny, charismatic, always knew what to say when.

He was very well known in the community and was a very generous person.

People were always knocking on our door for donations, and my father always taught us to share with others when we were able.
He was the ultimate role model.
That's why It hurt me so much that when I tried to talk to him about what had transpired he had no idea how to react.

The fateful day I found the courage to find words to share what I have been hiding for so long came along.

It Happened When I was 12 preparing for My bar mitzvah.

Sitting in the living room with my mom and dad late one night, We were going through the planned event details for the traditional celebration and I saw her name on an invitation.
It triggered me and I broke down.
I sat there for a good while just crying uncontrollably and my mom looked at my dad and my dad looked at my mom and they had no idea what to do.

We had this 2 room apartment connected to our basement that was empty at the time and my father took me downstairs to calm down while he went back upstairs.

Probably to talk with my mom?

He came sometime later and brought orange juice.

Sitting with my father in the basement of my house, I told him everything.

He just sat there in shock.
He went white and that scared me.
He tried to console me but what was he supposed to say?
He had no idea how to deal with this just as I did.

He promised me he would do something about it and even sent me to a therapist once who asked me a ton of questions and made me feel very uncomfortable.

He was the go-to for things like this in the community.

I soon found out that he was sharing details with my school because one day I was called into the dean of the school's office and he locked the door.

Locked doors scared me and I started sweating and getting queasy.

He stood close to me and took my hand in both of his and started rubbing it.

"Yossi," he said,

"Do you ever have certain feelings about people you can't explain?" he asked me.

My head started spinning.

Something didn't feel right and I became very uneasy.

I tried to pull my hand from his grip but he held it tight and looked into my eye.

I could smell the fish he ate for lunch on his breath.

"No" I meekly answered.

He looked at me with an amused look in his eye.
He stared at me, and his look was making me very uncomfortable.

I've seen that look before.

In the mikvah (ritual bath) every morning when he'd be there together with all of the students.

I felt betrayed.

This was the first of many betrayals I'd experienced from adults as a Teenager.

The next question made me very nervous:

"Do you know how to masturbate? He asked.

I did not know what that means yet but something in the way he said it made me stiffen up at the question.

I panicked.

I got up from the chair I was sitting in and frantically undid the lock.

The door clicked open and I bolted out of his office.

I spent the rest of that period in the school kitchen, googled, and found out that word he said was sexual, and it freaked me out.

My mind went into a frenzy as I tried to make some sense of what had happened in his office.

I was overloaded.
I was struggling badly with this reality.
I was not aware at the time but I had PTSD.

I spent a lot of time figuring out What the meaning of rape was, and recounting the specifics of what she had done to me, by googling literal terms of her actions.

After doing research using terms I picked up from one google search to the next, I learned that I was raped.

All the stereotypes I was reading about confused me, and I had no one to ask or talk to.

Apparently, Rape was something stronger people did to weaker people.

Did that make me weak??

Chapter 4

My bar mitzvah celebration happened shortly after and the school year continued, but My struggles were not over yet.

My father got sick around this time and was diagnosed with Cancer.

It started as a cough, which turned into a purple inhaler going with him wherever he went.

The day we found out he was sick was the day my life went from bad to worse.

My father was such a class act.
Before he told my mom he was sick he took her on a cruise with him to the Caribbean.

Only after they came back did he break the news to her. My father always thought about others before himself.

He fell ill before he could do anything more to help me.

I had to step up to the plate and together with my younger siblings we did our best to keep it together.

While I was dealing with all of this I had begun to have flashbacks and relive those moments.

I would wake up in a cold sweat.

My entire life as I knew it was thrown upside down.
I don't remember much of my last year in elementary school, (I've deleted a lot of it and the feelings attached to them with EMDR) but what I do, I remember vividly.

A few months before my father got sick, his father had a stroke.

We had gone away for the weekend with my grandparents to their country house upstate, and my mom and dad stayed in Brooklyn with my twin brothers, who were about two at the time.

We came home late Saturday night and my father told us: "Zaidy" (grandpa) had a stroke.

My father was a strong man.

6'2, 235, Not much would get in his way.

To see him sitting there, hunched over, worried beyond, kind of freaked me out.

When I told him about the abuse and saw the same reaction, I mentally blocked him out as being a source of help.

Something I regret to this day.

The funny thing is, looking back my parents gave me everything they could and went above and beyond for our family.

My dad tried his best to hold off and not go to chemo for as long as he could.

The first day he came back from his treatments he looked beaten.

He went straight to bed and stayed there for a long time.

It scared me that my dad was not going to be there to help me through this.
It scared me that my dad was sick with something that doctors weren't sure how they would treat.

It scared me that my dad, the big, strong, tall man I knew slowly turned into a shell of the person I once knew.

His spirit was still there but he was tired and exhausted.

I was petrified.

I still had so many questions I needed answers to.

These questions would follow me in the next six years until I got the tools to confront the answers.

The year phased out and I was recruited to join a Mesivta high school in Staten Island.

This for me was a sense of relief because Once my father got diagnosed and began treatment, the entire sense of normalcy took on a new meaning.

The new normal meant My mom was either on her way to, from, or getting ready for an appointment with my dad, all while balancing a full-time job as a teacher.

A certain sense of uncertainty set in, and it drove me bonkers.

My dad was a well-known figure in the community, and my mother being the sought-after educator and coach she is, had a large group of friends, and acquaintances.

The moment we weren't able to conceal the fact that my dad was sick, offers of help started piling in.

Everyone wanted to help.

From dinners, toys for my siblings, and day outings, it took a lot of the burden off my mom's shoulders as we were processing what was happening.

Order as we knew it fell apart and I had no one to turn two. It forced me to deal with things on my own, and This is when I figured out how important structure was and started trying to find ways to implement changes in my life. I needed to be there for my siblings and help out as much as I was needed.

Maybe now I'd have some time to deal with myself.

I needed someone to talk to and I tried to talk with one of the older boys I got to know at the school.

He asked me if I had ever been to therapy.
I had been to a therapist once (before all of this started) when I was younger because the camp I was going to wanted a Psychologist to sign off on me before I went.

They heard from my principal that I was not a good fit for their exclusive summer program. Gee, I wonder why.

That Got me thinking, so I looked him up.

That particular psychologist was a family friend and I found his phone number in the phone book.

I gave him a call and the next Friday, instead of doing my usual Mivtzoim (Chabad outreach) route,
  I traveled from the school on Staten Island to his home office in Brooklyn.

His rates weren't cheap and I had tried to start a business selling haircuts in school to pay for it.
I was always selling things to support my other habits,

and it made the most cents given I was in a boarding school with 50 teenagers.

Sitting in therapy for my first session, I instantly regretted coming. Try as I might, I could not get the words out.

I spent the session bawling my eyes out and he just sat there and handed me tissues.

On my third session, I had built some sort of confidence and had started sharing with him what had happened.

During that time, there was an older student who had managed to convince everyone to get haircuts through him instead of me and come the next week, I couldn't afford to pay for my session.

We came up with a payment plan, and after a few sessions, we agreed that I'd pay him the next time I came.

I had to delay for two weeks and things started to go downhill from there.

I started my own learning schedule in the school because I found myself frequently bored.

I came up with a system to add extra learning during review time, and the dean wouldn't hear of it.

I started acting out around this time and slowly started testing the limits.

I did not conform and he hated it.

He would constantly find me outside the "boundaries" we were allowed to go away from the school.

At Dunkin Donuts, CVS, or even the corner store.

One time he busted me with some food I had bought that did not have proper kosher certification.

He drove me back to my dorm and told me if it ever happened again I'd be expelled.

I could care less.

At the end of the day, I got good grades and knew my shit.

One day he came flying into the study hall and when he saw me doing my own thing he went off on me. Staying busy was one of my coping mechanisms to stay away from thinking about my flashbacks that kept me up at night.

"You can't keep to a schedule here, you'd be lucky to get a job in McDonald's – Because even there you need to keep a schedule," he yelled.

After about three minutes of ranting, he got into his car in front of the building and drove off.

I was burning mad. Here I was using my time to sit and learn, and I also helped out with meal service and other things they needed.

He would use the region on me to point out my flaws.

It planted a seed in my head that over the next three years would bring me through all sorts of hell.

As the year progressed, I fell into a depression.

I stopped showing up on time and most days would come in much after the morning prayers.

The rest of the year passed in a blur and I spent the summer up in the yeshivah program in Napanoch NY, which was run by one of the heads of the yeshivah and another rabbi.

It was here that for the first time In my life I had heard the term "self-help".

The rabbi who ran the camp had caught on that something wasn't right and called me into his office and asked me to tell him what was bothering me.

He kept on asking me to go deeper and deeper into my problems, cajoling me on.

Eventually, I told him about some of the things going on inside me.

It was a mindfuck.

Chapter 5

I started telling him that I was struggling with religion. He listened to me and started telling me that these are because of problems I have with internet addictions and this summer I'd have time to work and develop myself both the mind and soul.

I was grateful for those two months.

That summer I got drunk for the first time.

Every Thursday night we would have what's called a "farbrengen" A Chassidic gathering of the minds used to talk about self-development and furthering our connection to god and the rebbe (the Hassidic spiritual leader).

To achieve a workable state of mind everyone would take a shot of vodka.

Giving minors alcohol should be illegal - but I guess when used for a godly purpose it becomes ok?

I really liked the numbness the alcohol gave me.

After I drank enough of it I felt really strong.

Alcohol gave me the courage to think about things I normally wouldn't and talk about things I normally hid,

I'd get drunk at night and sit on the roof of the dorm recording into my iPod.

I spent a lot of drunk nights crying near the stream behind the building.

By the time it got to the end of the summer, my life just became a blur.

To me, it seemed like My life was rapidly going downhill and I couldn't seem to stop it.

School starting again didn't help it.

The first three months of my second year in Staten island were hellish.

They had changed up some rules and Took away my set of keys to the building.

They sat me down and told me that I had to follow their system.

That they had rules and if I wanted to stay at the school I'dd have to follow them.

Reasonable, But to me, that was a battle cry:

Going back to school triggered me in some way and I started having flashbacks again.

To make matters worse, after two months at school they found my iPod.

I had taken it with me that year to school for a lot of reasons, mostly to keep my google page open and be able to keep learning about myself while I was there.

I tried to explain to the rabbi when he confronted me but he wouldn't hear of it.

He was convinced I had a porn addiction.

And I'll give it to him, He was kinda right.

At the time this happened my father was still recovering from his surgery and was in and out of the hospital all the time. I was freaked out by the idea of him telling my father, and when I saw my dad pull up the next day to yeshivah and talk to the rabbi, I knew something was up.

My dad and I went for a drive, and he started laying in to me.

Turns out the therapist I hadn't paid called my dad and told him about it. There was also a family that called my dad and told him they had me on camera using a credit card I had cloned to buy alcohol from one of the local liquor stores.

Basically, I'd call in an order, use the card, and walk-in and pick it up.

Ballsy, I know.

Looking back Sometimes I think I'm lucky to be alive.

So many stupid decisions were to be made in the next three years, and this is just the beginning.

In a way, I am lucky that I never went to jail because of who my family was. Any time I'd fuck up and someone would catch me, they'd call my dad and he'd talk with me. The thing is I fucked up rarely, and when I did, my father was too weak to hash it all out with me.

I was heading down a dangerous slope.

This time it was different.

To top that all off, my dad had just found out that I had an iPod in school. The principal told him he was convinced I was addicted to porn, and my father went along with it.

All the time he was talking, my father and I sat in silence, and then when he was done we headed out of his office towards the car.

After a few minutes, my father informed me of his decision:

We were going to go back to that therapist and work this out.

I looked back at my dad and told him no.

No way in hell was I going to go back to that guy.

He had betrayed my trust and put me in all this shit.

My father got upset at me, the look of hurt very visible in his pained expression.

" We do everything we can for you. We work hard to provide for you and your siblings, and all we ask is for you to be good at school. Here you are not being honest and trying to steal from, the principal says your grades dropped and you have an iPod?!

WHAT IS WRONG WITH YOU? "

I felt so ashamed.

He was right.

I was a fuckup.

Although I was generally very good at school and had good grades which Are The very reasons why I was recruited here in the first place - when all of this went down none of it mattered to anyone.

Here I was going from a straight-A student to a troublemaker, I understand why they were so distraught.

Maybe had the principal taken a minute to think about what would cause someone to be so deceptive and had e healthy to have the talk with me things might have ended differently.

I don't know and will never find out.

We sat there for a moment in silence and then my survival mechanism kicked in.

I desperately just tried to shut all of this out and make it disappear.

I got out of his car and just walked away.

My mind started eating itself alive.

I had embarrassed my father, Stressed him out for no reason.

I don't conform.

I'm not good enough.

The events of the past few weeks and what had just happened weighed heavily on me.

I was going to get a drink. Drown it all out and go to sleep.
I had a secret stash I used to keep in the toilet tank in the dorm.

The ten-minute walk from the yeshivah building to my dorms was done from muscle memory. I was so numb from all these feelings I just wanted to feel better.

Is this ever going to end?

As I started drinking I started thinking deeper and deeper into the events of my life and really asking myself if it really was all worth it.

I had zero self-worth.
I was depressed,
I very strongly relied on alcohol to get through the day.

I felt hopeless.

I went to my dorm and sat on my bed.

" This is it"

I told myself. I can't deal with this anymore.

I stuffed my mouth with as many pain killers that I could fit in and washed it down with a cup of Smirnoff.

Then another.
Then another.

I felt so good. I was back in control. This time for the last time.

Goodbye pain, See you never.

You won, I lost.

My head started to spin, and my eyes watered over. I blacked out.

Hopefully for the last time.

It was all a blur when I woke up.

This happened Thursday night and so I spent the weekend in my bed, stuck in my own head. I felt like a zombie and didn't know what to do with myself.

It seemed like Life kept showing me that no matter what I did, I was not going to succeed.

 I sat there lost in thought just thinking.

I felt alone.
I felt scared.
I felt helpless.

Even though I missed the last few weeks of yeshivah, I still managed to get into the summer program. I knew I wasn't going back next year so I brought my iPod and a phone and made sure I had a steady supply of alcohol there.

How I managed and what went down those months is a book within itself, but let's just say I left the summer with a "fuck this" mindset.

I needed space.

I needed freedom.

I set out looking for a way to accomplish that and rid myself of my life as it had become.

Chapter 6

Questions are a very powerful thing.

From a very young age, children are very inquisitive and are always exploring their surroundings and environments in order to learn more about them.

As they learn more words, they start forming sentences and are able to verbalize their questions. Critical thinking develops in their brains as they start doing things more with curiosity.

Using their past experiences, the existing knowledge they have from said experiences, and the problem-solving skills they developed they are slowly able to start understanding things like the perspectives of others, compare and contrast and make simple the meaning behind things.

It is these skills that help children make decisions on a bigger scale as they grow up and are exposed to more real-life situations because they use their past experiences to determine and understand future outcomes of the same action.

The ability to read between the lines, understand the reasons behind things, slowly translates to unraveling the complexities of interpersonal communication, to make decisions on what to do next based on what they want their outcome to be.

The more intense my last experience was, the deeper my understanding became of how future experiences will play out.

Literally from the day you enter the world your brain is starting to develop these critical habits. Critical habits that developed themselves from real-life survival situations.

Although I am not an expert on the brain, I've studied a lot about this one particular organ and dedicate at least fifteen minutes every day to develop it.

With time I learned how to reprogram my thought process and did and continue to do a lot of work on my critical thinking process and intellectual affluence.

Most people don't know that you have three brains.

1. Your Head brain.
2. Your Heart brain.
3. Your Gut-brain.

Most people also don't know that your actual brain has three parts.

1. The Neocortex (Big Tex) - responsible for planning, understanding concepts,
abstract like thinking.
2. The limbic (Mid) Brain - responsible for social relationships, and emotions,

3. The Crocodile ("Croc") brain.

The crocodile brain is the most protected part of your brain and is also the most diverse.

It's the part of the brain that deals with survival, new situations, fight or flight, fear, and sex. It's attracted to the new and novel.

Learning how to use each of these systems, how they were intended, and practicing the exercises will give you complete control over your mind.

The Croc ("Reptilian") part of the brain's operating system has very little and very limited processing power

It also has a short attention span, that it guards very closely.

Therefore, as a result, it causes it to view new ideas as a threat to its state of survival.

It's also focused on flashy type things,
i.e. if something looks boring, it ignores it.

On that very same note, If something looks complicated, it radically summarizes what it is and then discards it.

Playing such a big part in development and survival, the Crock brain learns to adapt very quickly, and soon habits form.

The brain already starts understanding things and making decisions from the moment the baby is born.

This is why things that may have startled the baby like the sound of a door opening or closing it, slowly start becoming the norm and aren't processed as a threat anymore.

As it grows older and realizes that the sound of the door is what makes it possible to go from one room to the other, the thoughts are then passed along to the limbic system to determine what the next step is in the decision-making process.

Whether to open the door, to open the door and leave the room, to close the door after leaving the room, how to close the door, SO many Mini decisions leading up to an action.

This is why children and even adults are attracted more to bright colors, live presentations, grand performances, maybe even why people like clubbing.

Keeping decision-making minimal gives for an opportunity to relax, and take in the moment.

As I grow older I realize people like these things because it gives them an opportunity to "Dumb out" and just enjoy the moment.

The funny thing about Humans, while being the most ingenious creators on the planet we are also imitation machines.

You and I both have definitely seen an instance or two where someone went out and did something stupid, and lots of the (M)asses followed.

- **Social media fame.**

- **The fear of being different.**

- **Peer pressure.**

These are just some of the things that might have played a part in these situations.

In general, we imitate the habits of the groups:

1. The Close - What are friends and family doing?
2. The Many - What is the crowd doing?
3. The Powerful - What are those with influence doing?

This is true with everything that's been accepted as a social norm.

Religion is no different.

On the contrary, religion is a prime example of what a leader with a following can achieve.

When the powerful influence the many, the many will generally influence the close.

Look at the history.

Judaism, Christianity, Muslims, Sikh, Hindu, monk.

The common denominator with all of these religions regardless of how they practice is that they all follow a leader.

The leader they choose to guide them can come up with some radical idea and write it off that it was perpetuated in the name of religion.

This is more rampant with radical religious zealots and with all respect due, every religion has them and has people that were affected by them.

Matter of fact with religion in the mix a lot of the critical thinking that was supposed to take place at a very young age gets tainted as the years go by with the religious rhetoric that's used by some when questions are asked.

Most of the answers I have received up until this point in my life have been something along the lines of:

1) This is what God wants and this is how he wants us to do it.

2) This is a tradition.

3) This is just how it's done.

These were and still are a lot of the replies I get when I ask fundamental questions on the belief I was raised with.

Nothing wrong with my parents choosing to raise me the same way they grew up on. Matter of fact the quality of life growing up was really amazing.

I never felt like I was missing anything but also never felt like I had anything excessive. My parents are very modest and raised me as such.

Looking back, the first few years of my life were actually complete bliss.

Chapter 7

Rabbis of Olde don't like questions, especially the type about God, Jewish values, and religious views.

At least not the ones I had when I was in yeshivah.

As I moved along up in the yeshiva school system I saw this more and more.
A system that people blindly followed.
Not necessarily because it made sense, but because it came from the authority so there was nothing to question.
When someone dared to challenge something they were given answers of the similar style above or just straight up scolded for asking questions.

From the day that I woke up after the night I tried to end my life, none of it mattered to me anymore.

I did not care who God was or what he wanted me to do.

A wave of deep anger had started to form inside me, and it would only get bigger.

A dangerous depression had just shown itself and I had no idea what it even was to be able to deal with it.

A constant state of panic began to overtake me. Fear that I'd stay like this forever and never have a chance at being happy.

I felt like damaged goods, and that there was nothing I could do to change that.

Everywhere I went things wouldn't go as I wanted them to, try hard as I might.

My Mind took over and thus began the toxic cycle.

 Fuck, man.
I even tried to kill myself and failed at that.

There can't be anything I'm good at.

Here I was stuck in circles trying to figure out how to get out of these endless downward spirals I kept experiencing.

Why do these things keep happening to me?!

I'd ask myself every time.

What I would fail to do was look at the cause and effect and the true reason behind why things kept turning out as they did.

I'd always find ways to pin blame on other people every time and situation.

I felt like everyone was out to get me, and I needed to get away.

Over the course of the next few months, I was more trying to figure out how to do things outside of the yeshiva than I was trying to excel inside of the system.

Life had taught me that letting others determine and decide what I was capable of wasn't going to get me anywhere, and I committed to finding something that would help.

The problem was I kept fucking up.

I didn't know much and felt lost.

I was trying to start my own life up again on my own terms, each time I started something kept coming up.

After the summer was over and the new school year started, I now found myself with nowhere to go.

When it came time to come back for the third and final year the yeshivah decided it was better for me to find another place to study.

And with good reason.

Honestly, I was grateful I did not have to go back there. This had all become too much.

I was constantly clashing with my dad while I was home and I felt like being a 9-hour drive away from home would ease the tension a little bit.

Life had taught me early on that letting others determine and decide what I was capable of wasn't going to get me anywhere, and I committed to finding something that would help.

The problem was I kept fucking up.

I didn't know much.
I mean, why would I?

it's not like they teach that stuff in school anyways lol

I was trying to start my own life up again on my own terms, and it seemed to me that each time I started over again, something kept coming up.

With the new developments, I had no place to go to school.

To me, it felt like another attempt to sabotage my efforts.

This was supposed to go down without a hitch because it was considered an embarrassment to get kicked out of a school like this. Picture someone you know getting kicked out of Harvard. It's that bad.

The thing is that I was owed money from the school for work I had been doing on the side, and extracurricular programs to learn certain books by heart.

 I was in second place for earnings, and If they would kick me out, there would be no way for me to get that money.

This felt like a repeat of something similar that had happened to me once before, in a sleepover camp when I was 10.

 I was on top of the board for all of those programs, and they found a reason to disqualify my results.

I felt like I had realized that there are people in the world that just don't give a shit but make themselves happy and cover their own ass.

There had to be a better version of this all. That can't just be it.

To make matters worse, my father wasn't doing well, and over the course of the summer and beginning of fall, he had been in and out of the hospital and spent a lot of time at home.

Which meant he was on my case.

He had found some alcohol, cash, and a phone in my room over the summer, and he demanded to know what was going on.

This wasn't the first time he had found things in my room that I shouldn't have had, and each time it would end up in a fight and him yelling at me because I wasn't being straightforward with him.

The tension in the air was thick, and I needed to get out.

I would barely come upstairs from my room and when I did, it was to leave the house to go to a learning center – which was my cover for a good few hours – I'd either hop on a train and go to Atlantic Ave, or hang out behind the building and smoke cigarettes.

At that time, smoking cigarettes was literally my second most favorite thing in life after getting drunk. However, I hadn't started hardcore smoking yet. They were really hard to cover up in NY because when it's cold they smell even stronger.

I was still figuring it out.

I had tried them a few times and ironically my first time was with a nurse outside the hospital where my dad was one night when I stayed over.

I was going crazy with the way things were at home.

I figured, if I managed to get myself accepted to a school outside of NY, I'd have more freedom and be able to figure myself out.

There was a yeshivah in Toronto, headed by a rabbi who I knew from hanging around my cousins, and I figured if I had any shot in going anywhere, this was it.

I got his number and called him.

Our conversation lasted all of about five minutes.

He asked me what I was learning and I told him to test me on whatever he wanted. He asked me a few questions and told me to email his secretary.

I was in!

HOLY SHIT I DID IT!

I just taught myself something very important in life - you'll never know if you don't try and if you try you never know you might succeed.

This wasn't supposed to be this easy but I was grateful for it.

Whether it was a good thing or a bad thing that I was accepted so quickly, I didn't care.

I ran upstairs and told my parents I was accepted.

Two days later I got on to a bus from NYC, and nine hours later I was in Toronto.

New people, new places, most importantly new me.

It wasn't until later in my life that I realized I can be myself and not have to justify it.

I just needed to be validated.

And, I needed money.

Since I had shown up two weeks late, I never got any introduction to anybody. I just kind of went with it.

Before I continue, I need to set the tone for how this year went down, because it changed me on so many levels.

Chapter 8

The problem with the "system" is that everything is somehow connected.

I got stuck trying to explain it and skipped over and came back.

Here I am, and I am going to illustrate this with a story.

I had found a study partner who was kind of on the same page of checking out that I was. At least in terms of learning. He and I would spend the good first half of the session making Irish coffees and sitting in the middle of the study hall bull shoving and having a good time. Two parts liquor one part coffee. The cups stank up the room. LOL. The head of the school, our rabbi used to come over to our table and ask what was in the cups.

He knew what was up.

One day we were buzzed enough to make him one too. He smiled, tasted it, and told me to add more sugar.

Life was fun.

It was here that even more confusion began to set in.

For the most part of the past two years, I was living a double life. Looking back now I realize I was way ahead of myself. I didn't know it yet, but that's what it was.

I had no tools to communicate or do anything the "real world" would care about.

I was the perfect product of the "system".

I was stuck. The only talents I had were learning ancient teachings in-depth, explaining myself to the "mashgiach" (a term used to refer to the supervisor of the lesson – usually one of the teachers) , getting my way out of punishment, and being drunk without bothering too many people.

There were two main things on my mind most of the time.

- A) Being that I was in Toronto and alcohol was expensive, I needed to find someone who could get it for US prices.
- B) I needed to make money to be able to buy alcohol.

Very soon I realized I could become the guy who brought the alcohol through the border, and then resell it to the students in school once we reached Toronto.

Alcohol was a main staple in this school's DNA. Over the course of the 20 or so years the school was around, the Rabbi had developed an ulcer due to excessive drinking. Every year he spent three or four days after every Hasidic holiday in the hospital.

I figured out a system to bring in the booze, and I did that a few times when I went into NY.

I had someone meet me at the bus on its way to Canada and I would repackage the Smirnoff boxes and make them look like books.

The money rolled in.

Once we crossed the border into Canada a bottle went from $22 to $48.

I was hooked.

It sucked when I sold out because it would be four months before I headed back to NY.

I uncovered a few things I had not learned yet; People will pay for things they want.

In other words, the rule of supply and demand.

I started looking for things I could sell to people and make some money from.

With the money I made selling the Smirnoff, and also selling some newly released books bought on credit from a book vendor back home, I bought my very first phone.

I had heard of these lists called Craigslist and Kijiji that people would buy and sell things on it.

Now that I had a phone and a data plan, I downloaded the app.

I still had a few dollars left in my pocket from the phone purchase, and I started learning the art of buying and selling on craigslist.

Three days later I dipped out during a class and bought my first item. Then I was on another bus to sell the item to another customer on the other side of town.
That day I made $119 dollars and learned a lot about the Toronto public transportation system.

I thought I had it all figured out.

Not before Life was about to teach me another lesson, or five.

The kid I bought the phone from was a shady character, still is to this day.

(I got like eighty friends named Mendy but dude, you know who you are and you're going to get caught one day. I promise.)

I didn't care, though. So long as the phone was unlocked and I'd be able to use it to make more sales I was happy.

I was starting to get the hang of it until one day I bought three pairs of beats from a dude who pulled up to my dorm and popped them out of his trunk. I paid like $30 a pair and was too dumb to ask or check f they were real.

I went back to the school and sold them to some younger kids for $65 a pair and made some nice profit. I went for a smoke and drink on my way back to the dorm that night and I was all happy.

What would happen tomorrow would change my view on everything I thought I had known up until this day.

The morning started up as usual.

Got to school at seven, hung up my coat (with my "illegal" phone in the zipper pocket), and forgot about it til about 12- noon. When I got bored I would usually take my phone out of my coat and hide it in my pants. Then I'd go to the bathroom and start hunting for deals.

Just like usual, I went to the back to pull my phone out of my pocket.

It wasn't there.

Chapter 9

I panicked.

My biggest fear was that one of the staff had found it and I was about to be shipped back home. Just when I had begun to slowly set something up for myself.

A few very tense days.

 Each time someone from the faculty staff walked in I was half ready to get called to the Rabbi's office and have to answer my phone.

Until someone came over to me and shared with me what some of the friends from the older classes saw.

Some of the older kids had noticed him using the very same iphone he sold me at a place we used to catch the internet signal from apartment buildings near the dorms, and the kid hadn't been around the school in a few days. Worst part for me, he was the head rabbi's nephew. I was faced with a choice. Do i do something right now that could potentially get me kicked out of school forever if i was wrong or do I wait til he eventually shows back up and might have already gotten rid oit?
I had no choice but to go back to the dorm and start looking for him.

Someone must have let him know I was coming because his light was still on but his room was empty.

This idiot forgot to turn off the ringer, and I ended up smashing in the bathroom door near his room and grabbing the phone from his hand. We fought it out and I came out on top. He had a bashed face and tore his pants. After talking to him, He told me he wanted the phone back. I took him to the bank where he got me back my money.

Another lesson learned: Never trust nobody, Ever.

I went the next day to the Apple store and got another phone.

At my best time hustling I was selling about 2-3k worth of electronics a week and making decent money for a kid my age with no expenses.

The Problem was I had bills.

At this point I was smoking about 2 packs a day and was getting drunk every night.

I started up some new side hustles. I was still doing haircuts, but I was ramping up electronic sales, and sold a bunch of religious items I bought for cheap to the kids in the school. I also had American cigarettes that were brought in as often as possible.

$43 at duty free, became $65 or even $80 if you sold right.
I would sell them to classmates, or bring them to the local Chinese bodega and make a few dollars a pack.

Canadian cigarettes are shit.

At one point I decided I would try to talk to one of the therapists in the community and see if maybe I would be able to figure myself out.

That ended up with an invite to his house for a Shabbat meal one Friday night where we all drank and ate and after everyone left I shared my struggles with him. After that things got weird. Therapy was never going to work out so I just took what came to me in stride and rolled with it.

I got the rap as a "go to" for most anything guys needed and technically, I was already comfortable in that role. It was only a few months ago I was the hookup for alcohol and smokes on the streets in Crown Heights.

I was missing classes, but at the same time stacking cash.

Later on that year one of my classmates passed away, and I took it upon myself to build a library in his name.

I got a list of names and numbers from the school admin and called every parent asking for a donation. Without knowing it at the time, I had put in place a lead Generating system to keep track of everything, and after all was said and done I raised over 40K for that library.

It was too bad that the institution wasn't cash flow positive when It came to cashing the checks.
The system we set up was simple.
I would get the donor to fill out a check in the school's name, or they would give me a credit card number for the school secretary, who would then process it and was supposed to keep a balance sheet of payment received.

Maybe if I had checked in with her everyday things would have been different. Then again, probably not.
When the time came to head back to New York to go pick up all of the books it was my horror to find out that she had forgotten to track the last few payments I had sent her and didn't log two really big checks I had received the month before.

Another lesson learned here about trusting people to do their job.

I sat in her office for almost four hours going through all of the donations that came in for the school and watched with frustration as the 40K in payments I had fundraised became 19K and after the exchange rate was factored in I had about 12K.

I started to see a pattern with certain things in the system, one of them being money and anything that had to do with it.

It was either lost, made, hidden, or flashed. No one talked about it though, you'd kind of hear it through the grapevine.

On the one hand I was pisse., I had poured a lot of energy into raising the funds and wanted it to be one grand library. On the other hand it gave me more leverage and a reason for the Rabbi to avoid talking to me. I was slowly missing more and more classes, and quite frankly it seemed like they could care less.

Everything was great.

Chapter 10

Back when I was in yeshiva in Staten Island, there was a group of kids two grades older than me that acted like they were the shit, and had a super inner circle type clan thing going.

Me being the loud mouth I was, had frequent run-ins with those kids, and one time this kid, (ironically also named Mendy) shoved me up against a wall, and tried to pat me down and see if I had a set of keys to the building. I was a big kid, 5'8 maybe 200 pounds. No way I was going to let this kid run me over like that. We had a little fight, and let's just say the rest of the year he found other kids to pick on.

Of all places to have skipped a grade and go to another school. I ended up in the SAME SCHOOL as this fucker.

My luck.

I found myself stuck and being called out for stupid things whenever he had a chance. He was the only thorn in my side. I don't know what I ever did to deserve it, but shit like that is what ate at me.

I kept on being reminded that I was in what seemed to be a dog eat dog world. I felt uncomfortable being in that room, and did my best to keep out of it.
Then I found out his family supported the school.

This kid one time decked a younger student in the face, and the Rabbi didn't do much about it.

His dad was part of some Mafia in NY. You don't mess with the mafia.

It took me some time but after a while I learned that if you stopped giving them shit to throw at you, then you don't have anything to throw at you and move on to someone else.

At that point in the year I had made friends with one of the guys, and we formed this sort of brotherhood if you will. He found out I smoked, and he smoked too, we were also both borderline alcoholics.
Things were looking up.

Looking back, that year for me was kind of just what I needed. To air out and make my decisions for the coming year. I was about to make a mistake so big, I thought I'd be done for.

I had no previous experience or knowledge of running a business and somehow I managed to get four ventures going in about 5 months that were all bringing in money. I started looking for more ways to make money. Something that got me in trouble all through middle school.

One day I watched a kid get on the phone and call a detergent company to complain, and he got a $200 Visa card. Cash. Holy shit that was crazy! I knew it was some shady shit but I HAD to give it a shot.

Three weeks later I had over $1000 in free cash, shoes, and coffee delivered to the yeshiva building. I was hooked. Over the course of the next few weeks, Me and my boys got over 5k worth of "scammed" goods from various companies.

I was this big loud kid in school that everyone knew could hook them up with whatever they wanted. When the challenge was put in front of me to get it done, in order to show that I could, I would get it done.
We both did it together.
Till today there are may be 3 or 4 people that I can truly call friends.

I attribute this to my childhood and instinct, but for some reason I was always trying to please people. I had never learned anything about human emotions and did not know that this was detrimental. I just wanted them to accept me and would go to almost any limit to make them happy. A doormat, if you will.

No matter how low things get, never allow yourself to become other people's doormat. I lost a part of me again and would only pick back up later.

Chapter 11

One day I'm standing in the back of the building on my brand new iphone trying to set up a deal.

There are three entrances to this huge building and everyone usually only used the front two.

This was my usual spot to dip out of the study hall for a quick two minutes since it was close to the entrance of the hall, but also around a corner so I was out of sight. Suddenly the door opened behind me and Rabbi K - The rabbi overseeing that particular lesson - popped in. He saw me just as I was shoving the phone into my pants pocket. He looked at me with a stern look and stretched out his hand as if to say " Give me the Phone". I wouldn't even entertain the thought of handing it over so he stuck his hand into my pant pocket and took the phone from me.

No phones were allowed in the school, and they usually never gave them back if they caught you.

Fuck my life.

I'm out $900 Bucks, and needed to find a way to make it back.

I found myself in front of the Dean, and managed to convince him to give my phone to my dorm counselor. I sold the dorm counselor on the idea that I'm going to return my phone to Apple, and even created a label as if I had an Apple return label.

I paid the guy off at the UPS store to hold the box, and told my dorm counselor to just drop it off there and give him a confirmation number. To my happy disbelief he dropped it off, and one hour later I had my phone back.

I got drunk that night and replayed what had happened that day in my head.

I was so proud of myself for being quick on my feet and not losing my composure when it came to figuring this out and coming up with a solution.
I had outsmarted them and they had no idea.
It was such a good feeling.

The exact feeling is hard to describe.

I felt like for the first time, I had control.

Not like the way alcohol gave me control though. This was a completely different sort of feeling.

I wanted to figure out ways to feel in control of things.

Keeping busy was always one of my coping mechanisms. It drowned out the constant buzzing in my head.

I was in a really dark place.

Experiences like these had shown me that If I wasn't going to do this and stand up for myself then no one would.
I was just another name on a list of people who had managed to get into this yeshivah just like I was the last one.

It's a numbers game over here.

No one actually cared.

Unless of course I was late. In which case I'd have to pay a $15 fine every half hour.

Paid in cash to the rabbi giving the class.
I must have spent upwards of $500 being late the whole year.
If the rabbi would have noticed something more than his own ego he'd see that I was almost always hungover when I came late. Because I was always drinking the night before.

I had finally found a way to silence the voices in my head at night and sometimes during the day.

I was so numb when I drank alcohol.
My brain would relax and I'd just lay there.

Thinking all sorts of random thoughts trying to figure out what the fuck.

Ever since I was raped I had a very distorted look on the world and its creatures.

For me there was no normal.

I had this weight I subconsciously carried around with me all the time that stopped me from doing things like everybody else.

I couldn't go to the Mikvah without feeling violated.
I couldn't look a woman in the eye and say a word.
Even if it was something as simple as a cashier in a grocery store.
I suffered from flashbacks and PTSD.

I'd wake up in a cold sweat in the middle of the night after reliving that devil woman sliding her dry fingers deep inside my body till I bled and begged for her to stop.

Looking back I have no idea why I hadn't come out sooner in order to get the help I needed quicker in order to be able to have a normal adolescent life. Normal by societal standards or whatever.
I had no idea what that meant, anyways.

I started to become very narcissistic.
 I believed the world was out to get me and I had to go to war first.
I was really worried about my dad and my family but I couldn't go back home and face them.
I felt so much shame.
I was trying everything I could to get more information on what the outside world was like in a search for something better.

Something I could do to get myself out of this.

Dealing with all of this trauma severely warped my perception of the world and combined with my lack of education, I was going to pay for it when I left the system on my own.

I really did not like the limitations this lifestyle had imposed on me.

I felt like I was stuck in between two broken worlds.

Part 2.

Personal accountability and self control.

Personal accountability is the cornerstone and one of the key components in the foundation of self development. If you cannot control yourself, who will?

I'll show you how I did it.

Chapter 12

The year slowly began coming to a close and I was looking forward to the summer.

My family was scheduled to go on a summer trip to Israel, and I was really excited.

I had never been there before and this would be the first time my parents, my siblings and I would go on such a trip together as a family.

Sure, we'd taken plenty of vacations together as a family, but this was different.
This was in order to celebrate my brother's bar mitzvah at the Western Wall in Jerusalem.

I was always interested in the history of the state, and had learned so much about it while growing up in school.

Finally the day came, it was time to leave this place to go on a summer trip to Israel with my family.

My brother Ari was going to have his bar mitzvah there. School wasn't supposed to end for almost a month but I got permission to leave two weeks early and bounce.

There was a small party held in the backyard of our house before I came back from yeshivah, and I felt really hurt that the family would choose to do something without me.

A bar mitzvah celebration is a big deal, and I would have loved to be there with my family and join in on it. Had I taken a moment long enough to calm down and understand the calculation I wouldn't have been as hurt and upset as I was, but I was too self absorbed just trying to survive that in all that noise - I was only thinking about myself.

When i finaly got home from school, I randomly started picking fights with my siblings over stupid things. This was more than just the normal sibling rivalry common among children. Maybe I was trying to make a point or maybe I was trying to share some of the hurt I was feeling inside. Because I did not know how to verbalize it, I did the second thing I knew best. Illustrate it with actions.

I was really unpleasant to be around.
I found problems with every little thing.
I made big mountains out of small molehills.

I am 11 years older than my youngest siblings.
In places I should have been acting as the bigger brother, I was acting like the biggest nuisance. Constantly complaining and just being a dick.

Even before we left for the airport my father had a stern talking to with me. One I deserved but instead took it as an attack.
He had no idea what was going on in my head, nor did my past experiences show me that I'd have any luck sharing it so I didn't bother.

It was here that I started to create a disconnect with my parents and my family.

It's a shame really that it took me so long to figure all of this out and for a long time I really regretted it. It caused me to really miss out on a golden opportunity and this wouldn't be the last of it.

My mom's entire family joined us.
My father masterminded the trip of a lifetime. What happened
throughout the 24 days we were there, is a book within itself.

One of the big things on my mind during this trip was my next year of yeshivah.

Similar to the traditional schooling system, yeshiva schools have six years of advanced jewish education divided into two sets of three.

I finished my first three years in this new system, and had set my eye on a really elite boarding school in France, that had a very prestigious name. For some reason or maybe because of the status of the schools I had been in I always felt that I needed to be in the best schools. I saw the jealousy in my old elementary school friends' eyes, when I was in my old school, and it gave me a sense of importance I wanted to maintain. I'll bet it was a self portrait. A sense of self importance. Let's be real no one actually gave it much thought when we were done speaking about it but this to me was one of my lifelines.

I convinced myself that I needed this.

I was a pretty good student, who somehow still had A/B grades.Once I convinced my parents to let me apply I waited eagerly for their acceptance letter.

One week went by, then another. Until one day my dad shared with me that they had called him with their response.

They deemed me unworthy of attending their school for the coming year after talking to the dean of my old school in Toronto.
The reason they gave was due to my behavior last year. They can't take the risk of me being there because they

dont want me to be a negative influence on the other guys in the school.

I was 16 at the time and hearing this enraged me.

I felt hurt that they didn't want to accept me.

I was really proud of myself and the things I did the last year and to hear someone call that negative, and to be worried about me recruiting other students to do things similar both made me sad and made me feel hopeless.

Was anyone able to view my accomplishments as a positive thing and not constantly telling me I needed to be better?

Why can't they just accept me for who I am and what I do?

I felt like everything was closing in on me.

I started panicking. Getting accepted here
after all the crap I had been through that led up to this, I needed a change that would propel me forward and not just try and nail me down to a system that I had to follow even if I didn't want to.

Around this time I started questioning.

Around this time I started questioning.

Questioning myself.
Questioning the people around me.
Questioning everything.

I was so confused as to what was going on both in my mind and in my life, that I stopped caring.

Chapter 13

I probably ruined the whole trip a few days in.

One night when I came back to our hotel, my Dad smelled cigarette smoke on me when I "came back" from the evening prayers, and got really mad at me.

My parents had a hunch that I smoked, but had never actually caught me in the act. This was the first time they had any sort of hint that I was a smoker.

The fact that I was even smoking at this time still puzzles me. I was literally living with a cancer patient who wasn't a smoker, yet still had been diagnosed with this cursed illness in his lungs.
 My dad was sick the whole year and the fact that he was even on the trip with us here in Israel was a miracle. I did not know it at the time but this would be the last opportunity we had together to travel as a family.

Being that our day was always filled with a packed schedule, by the time we came back to our hotel in the evening he was exhausted, and usually went to sleep after planning the schedule for the next day and making sure everything was in order.

It was expected of me to go to prayers with a minyan (Quorum of ten men) for prayers three times a day.

I would go to them by myself, and this usually gave me time to wander around and explore the city on my own.

After a while, I stopped going to them, and started exploring the city.

One evening, I walked past this man sitting at a cafe table on a street corner. I don't know what possessed this random guy to call me over, but once I found out he spoke english, we started talking.

The first few minutes I just stood there and spoke about random things. Then, things became more serious like religion and observance.

Israel, although being a Jewish state, has only a small percentage that are ultra-orthodox religious.

Walking around the streets with a black borsalino hat and suit jacket, instantly gave me away as hassidic.

To this day I do not know who this man is, but at the time, he was the only person who seemed like he was genuinely interested in me. He asked me to explain how was felt about religion. Usually, a touchy subject whenever we did outreach and one I usually stayed away from, but I felt comfortable enough to ask him questions.

I don't know what possessed me with the courage, or why this man was interested in listening to me, but I took everything at face value and was enjoying the conversation.

I had never had the opportunity to candidly discuss my beliefs without feeling like I was under attack, or the person was trying to convince me that I was wrong and he was right.

It felt really good to get all of my doubts off my chest, and this man just sat there and listened.
"If you want to try something new, well then why don't you?" He said.

I looked at my watch and alarmingly realized I was sitting here talking to this man for over an hour! Evening prayers usually took about fifteen minutes, and the walk back to the hotel was about ten, so I was over forty minutes late than when I was expected to be back.

I ran back to the hotel, and it was only after I had opened the door to our family suite that I realized I forgot to clean up the cigarette smell off my breath and face.

The hotel had a men's room right off the main lobby and I usually would wash my face and pop a breath mint after I snuck a cigarette most nights when we came back

to the hotel to sleep.
I was in such a rush back, that in my haste I forgot this seemingly trivial detail.

I opened the door and my dad was sitting on a chair in the dining room with my mom sitting next to him.

There was no way I was getting out of this one. So I braced myself and walked inside.

"Yossi," My father asked, ``Did you smoke a cigarette?"

"No." I answered. Lying straight to his face.

Lying was a bad habit I picked up already from when I was in my first year of school in Staten Island. It seemed like for the most part people bought them, so I kept on using lies to get myself out of sticky situations.

"Come with me to the porch," he said.
I tried to tell him I had to use the bathroom really badly, but he beckoned me outside.
I slowly walked outside and tried to keep my distance from him.
I had no idea what he was going to do and I was scared.

"I'm going to ask you again, and don't lie to me. Were you smoking cigarettes? "

My mind was thinking frantically.
 What should I say?!

Suddenly I remembered that I had lots of friends from school who were also in summer programs in Israel, and after a moment of silence, I replied.

"I don't know Ta." I answered while coming up with the next lie. My mind went into overdrive and my body slightly trembled.

My father never caught me red handed with anything, and when he confronted me in the past, I had always prepared a quick response that usually worked.

Maybe because he didn't want to fight with me or maybe because I actually succeeded in deceiving him, I will never know,

Nothing prepared me for this, and since I was caught off guard, I was struggling to reply with a sensible explanation.

I gulped and took a deep breath.

"I bumped into some friends on my way back from the prayers. They must have been smoking and the smell rubbed off on me." I said.

He looked at me with amusement, and lovingly told me something I still remember to this day:

"If you lie once, all of your past truths become questionable.
Since I'm your father, I love you unconditionally and even though I don't always understand you I will always support you.

One day you might lie to someone who will find out you lied to them and they will never trust you again.
Honesty is always very important because trust is never something you can earn back.
I only want the best for you and for you to lie to my face shows how disrespectful you've become.
I don't know where you actually went tonight, or if you even really went to pray.
Frankly, I don't know what to think.
If you keep up this behavior Mommy and I will be forced to send you back home early. "

Maybe it was the conversation I just had. These types of conversations that I never usually had with my dad, or the words he used that triggered me.

I, for some reason only heard that my father was telling me that he didn't trust me and wanted to send me home from the trip.

I felt attacked.

How could this man, who tells me that he loved me unconditionally, not see the pain I was going through?

Was he also out to get me?

We both walked Inside.

My survival mechanism kicked in and I shut him out the rest of the night.

I started skipping the prayers and instead would walk around Jerusalem aimlessly exploring the ancient but modern city.

I'd get lost in my thoughts.

As the trip progressed, it came to a point where no one could stand me, and I couldn't stand anyone.

I think everyone was relieved when I went to pray because it gave them some time to not have to deal with my constant negativity.

I became very bitter and my need to get away was getting stronger every day.

The last few days of that trip flew by in a blur.

Later on that week, we boarded the flight back home.

I had my own seat, on the opposite end of the plane then my family.

After I had a few shots, and settled into the rest of the 12 hour flight back home, I started to panic.

This whole time on the trip I hadn't done anything to find another yeshivah to go to or that would accept me.

The school year was quickly approaching and I had nowhere to go.
 I needed to work on a new plan. And quickly.

Chapter 14

After lengthy conversations with the rabbis at the school and thorough testing, I managed to get myself into a school in Montreal, and found out that to my luck one of my boys from Toronto was there
also..

I showed up to the school late November. Three weeks late to the year.
Because I had shown up late, I had everyone's leftovers, and ended up in a dorm where I was the only occupant.

I was used to this, because last year in Toronto it had been the same. I slept in a room of my own in the basement. That was one of the ways I was able to hide my alcohol so well.

I had put a deadbolt on my door so no one was able to get into it, and anyone who visited figured it was a storeroom and didn't ask questions.

Rather than choose to play victim to circumstances, this time I decided I would roll with it, and make this work.

Like last year, the basement I moved into worked out to my advantage.

Finally I'd have some peace and quiet.

The last three weeks I spent at home were literally a repeat of the same time I spent at home just a year before that.

The only difference was that I had grown more distant from my family.
I spent a lot of time in my room and on my phone.
I was consuming all the content I could.

I spent time watching videos on youtube, and reading books that were available for free online.

I also finally had the guts to watch a full porn video for the first time.
Once the video loaded and I started watching it I felt numb.
It really didnt do anything for me in the beginging because whenever I saw the actions being played in the video it reminded me about my rape.

I stayed up late every night, and learned things like how to splice internet, and how to make hiding spots in walls undetected.
I also watched videos on how to shoplift and get away with stealing things, but also watched videos about Repo teams and life in jail.

I was thirsty for information.

A week later, when I realized that I would be the only one on this side of the dorm for the year, I put my knowledge to use and connected to a neighbor's router with one of my own. After it was set up I wired it into the wall giving me unlimited wifi.
With all of the students in the school, I figured it would be forever until someone figured it out, and by then who knows what will be.

This was the beginning of my plan for the end.

I started working full time on figuring myself out.

I decided that now that I was here, I was going to figure out a way to leave this all once and for all, and start a new life somewhere out on my own.

I had zero skills to survive in the real world. I knew where I wanted to go, I just didn't know how to get there. I needed direction.

I kept reminding myself of the stories we'd used to hear, of Hasidic men running away from their wives and kids and starting a new life somewhere else in the world far away from their home.

These were my inspiration.

Not to ever run away from my family God forbid but I felt like I understood how someone would end up in a position like that.

I was feeling the same way.

I turned to my trusted information source on google, and began plugging away.

Slowly I began piecing my plan together.

At the same time, I also had to focus on keeping it together and maintain appearances so long that I was still here.
I wasn't religious at this point and did not observe anything.
I really needed to be careful not to raise any red flags and tried really hard to lay low.

Unlike last year, me and my friend were both given stern warnings that any single misbehavior we'd be thrown out for good.

I was there for about three weeks, when things started to get a bit better.

The school seemed to be very impressed that I was so advanced in learning, and the rabbi and I had begun to build some nice rapport.

Smoking in this school was against the rules, and anyone caught with a cigarette in hand was fined $100 cash.

Being a smoker, this was very hard for me especially as it started getting colder and the smell got stronger.
I'd smoke my cigarettes by sticking the butt into a plastic disposable fork, and would hold the stem of the fork from the bottom and smoke it like that.

I probably could have just waited until the end of the day when I did not have to go back to the study hall, but part of the thrill was going back into the study hall afterwards and no one being able to tell.

I cleaned up well after myself and kept all different kinds of colognes and candles in my room to cover up the smell.

The following week we were assigned routes to go out on Friday afternoon and do Chabad outreach work.

I got assigned to downtown Montreal which couldn't have been more perfect.

It was already early October, and as tradition, we would go out to shop owners and passerby alike, asking them if they wanted to perform a mitzvah of putting on tefillin in honor of the Jewish new year.
It was traditionally a somber time.

It was expected of us to get up earlier than usual, and recite "Selichot" (prayers for forgiveness) with a minyan in the study hall.

This was not the time of year to be acting up.

I managed to make it past my first month at school with no incidents.

I used the opportunities I got when they sent us on these outreach missions to go out with My Friend and we'd go spend a few hours together in a Starbucks. We'd kill the time using our phones without a care since we were far away from school.

There was also a custom that I had adapted from my last year in Toronto, that when in yeshivah, every Friday before sundown we would all get together and drink.

"A Bein" it was called.
Using the Hebrew words for sunset.

Some of my friends still do this together till this very day.

My Friend and I would always down a 1.5 liter bottle of labatt blue, and smoke cigarettes till we had to go to services.

He did not know it at the time, but a lot of the feedback he gave me from those talks helped me work up more and more to the reality of packing up my bags and leaving the system for good.

We would spend long nights smoking cigars in a park not too far away from the school, and talk about everything under the sun.
We did this for a few weeks and I felt like we were becoming really close friends.

In the beginning, when we first met in Toronto, it was weird to me, this friendship.

I wasn't used to people just caring about me because they cared, or wanted to talk to me because they were genuinely interested to listen and actually hear me out. This friend had taught me over the last year together that I could trust him, and l slowly began to open up to him about my struggles with my relationship with my parents and my life at home before yeshivah.

We both had similar issues with our parents in terms of feeling that they did not understand us, and talking about them really helped us get clarity on our next moves.

We were together all of last year and the fact that he ended up in Montreal with me really was a blessing.

I never before had someone I was able to consider a friend.

This friend meant alot to me.

One week, to go with the beer, we decided to make a meat stew.
 A jewish Ashkenazi food called "Cholent" made from potatoes and meat for our Friday night bein.

We went to the store and when we were shopping he dipped to the bathroom for a minute.

When we got back to the dorm out of his coat he pulled two huge packs of stew meat.

 I looked at him with disbelief but also a big respect.

This dude had just shoplifted like $50 worth of meat like it was no big deal.

I was in awe.

I had shoplifted before too but never like that.

We put up the stew Thursday night, and in the morning went out like our usual Friday afternoon routine to Starbucks.

When we came back the whole building wanted to know what we were making. We had made the concoction in my room, which was in the basement of the building next door to the room my friend was in. Since it was a duplex, and both buildings were connected over its life holding students had many holes in the walls, the smell had spread throughout the entire dorm.

Everyone all of the sudden wanted to come chill in my room. People who haven't so much as looked me in the face or even said hello since I got here over a month and a half ago all of a sudden we're coming to my room trying to hang out.

In reality, they just wanted to taste the food I made. Me, being socially awkward as hell, while also really wanting to be accepted by everyone gave the whole thing out.

I didn't even taste it.

I decided I was going to do the same thing again the next week, and then did it again the week after that.

Every week we would get more and more brazen.

Taking things of more value, adding more things to these Friday night parties.

Everyone who was in on it at school started looking forward to the weekend so we could all hang out together and eat and drink.

This year really looked like it was on the up and up.

Chapter 15

Friends are a really cool thing if you have the right ones.

The right friends are the people who actually don't want anything in return for being your friend and just appreciate you as the person you are.

They are in it for who you are, and not for what you can give them.

People who are constantly looking for ways they can get things from others for free because they are "friends" are snakes and dangerous people.
These people will suck you dry till your last drop and then keep sucking.

I was so desperate for validation and recognition that I really didn't care in the beginning where it was coming from, or the price I was paying to get it.
Anyone who thought I was cool would get showered with all sorts of gifts and random things because I was scared of losing their friendship.

This was the usual way I was used to getting friends.

Ever since I left for yeshivah for the first time back when I was 14, I used all sorts of ways to try and buy people's friendship.
Since I had no sense of self worth, I felt like there was

nothing inside of me that people would want to be friends with.

While others seemed to just naturally get along together, I struggled to make friends.

Why would someone want to be friends with me? I would ask myself. I don't have anything to offer them.

The rape had taught me that people always do things for something in return. It can't be just because they want to get to know me. I had no idea who I was and was really confused with social dynamics because of my flashbacks.

So I figured that if I offered things to them that they would want, then eventually they would be my friend because they liked the stuff I gave them.

It got to a point when it was really bad. Where I would literally do anything for attention and a feeling of acceptance.

I would steal in order to get things to share with others.

One time when I was 14, I spent $150 to order stuff to our school for a friend's birthday who I knew couldn't afford to make a party.

Whether I felt bad for him, or if I was just doing it so everyone would talk about it, was something I spent a lot of time self searching because I genuinely liked helping people but at the same time I really needed the credit and recognition when I did it.
I figured that if they would like the things I had, and the things I shared with them, then they would want to be my friends.

First it was small things like chocolate bars from the grocery store. Then things like the credit card I got busted for later on.

Since I was the only one who came from my school to be there, everyone already had their cliques and social circles already set up for them.

I made this my coping mechanism in yeshiva, and spent a lot of the money I was making on doing things for other people in order for them to like me.

Three years I'd been doing this, and usually, it worked every time.

I felt like I had this whole friends thing figured out.

I did not then know how flawed this mindset was and would not learn this life lesson until way later on.

It seemed like it worked in this school also. All of the popular kids would hang out with me every Friday night, and we'd eat the food I made and drank together.

One such Friday night, we were all sitting around in the basement when the door opened up and our mashgiach burst in.

Everyone was quiet, in shock that he was there.

He was the Rabbi of a local synagogue, and usually on Friday nights he was busy over at the shul and never came to check on us.
I still don't know if he knew this was going on and waited to see if it would continue or if he happened to come by for a random check up and was also shocked by what he saw.

Different from the last yeshivah I attended, in this school, I wasn't the only one who did not keep shabbat. Once we were all cool with each other we used our phones in my room openly and without caution.

What he saw made him very angry, and he started shouting.
"How is such a thing possible to be going on in my school! He bellowed.

"All of you are going to have a meeting with me when shabbat is over and you will all be punished! Desecration of shabbos is not tolerated here."

He took note of our names and saw the amount of empty beer bottles and the empty crock pot that was just before filled with meat and potatoes.

Whose is this? He asked.

"Mine",

I answered. Scared at what he would say next.
I was really hoping he didn't see my phone before I managed to shove it under the cushions, and even more so on a night like tonight.

Just like the rest of the yeshivas I attended, having a cellphone and not giving it in before it started, was grounds to be expelled in its own right, But this?
This would have made it a sure thing.

"Come see me tomorrow night at my house." He said, visibly angry.

That night I did not sleep. I was having extreme anxiety about what might happen.

Chapter 16

That Night I stayed up playing out the possible scenarios in my head.

I was here on a one strike trial. No ands, ifs, or buts.

I was so sure I was going to be sent home on Sunday that I started planning the story I would tell my dad when I had to call him and tell him I would be taking the next bus home.

Tears were streaming down my face, as I took my seat on the self pity train that just left the station heading to nowhere good.

I fell asleep for a few hours and woke up in a cold sweat.

I had a crazy nightmare and spent the rest of my day in my bed not wanting to go out or see anyone.

Word of the bust spread throughout the whole yeshivah.

That afternoon a few of the guys came to my room with a bottle of Smirnoff and some snacks.
We all did a few shots and I loosened up and started feeling a bit better.

I drank about another half cup, and we all started singing and having a good time.

Saturday night came, and I was getting ready to go to the rabbi's house.
I had no idea what was in store for me, so I did what I usually did before I had to go to something I was scared of. I smoked a cigarette, showered and brushed my teeth.

I put on fresh clothing and started the 5 minute walk to the rabbi's house.

As I was walking I heard my friend call out to me from a different direction : Yossi!! He called out, using my nickname for my Hebrew name - Yosef.

I turned around and smiled when I saw him.
He was holding up two white plastic shopping bags.
Inside those bags were a few slices of pizza, and two large containers of poutine.
A Canadian favorite that I really took a liking to.

I waited for him to cross the street and when he got closer to me he smiled and said: " make it quick at the rabbi's house. I got these for when you come back."

"Thanks! "I said, wow he really knew how to make me

feel better.

All of the sudden things didn't seem so bad and I continued walking in the direction of the rabbi's house.

When I got there, he was busy with a child emergency. I don't know how many kids he had, but it was around bedtime and he and his wife were both busy.

He told me he would come back to the school a bit later, and he would talk to me then.

"How bad could it be?" I thought to myself.
If I was going to be expelled he would have done that already.

When I got back, my friend and I went to my room. We sat down and enjoyed the food, and spoke about what had transpired over the weekend.
I asked him if he thought I'd get kicked out. He was caught before for similar things like this, and if there was anyone I knew who could give me advice on this subject right now it was him.

"Agree with him with anything he tells you you did, and after he's done talking try to talk to him like a human being and not the "Mashgiach" He told me.

This seemed so foreign to me. I was used to proving my point and making sure the person I was talking to understood what I was trying to say before I even heard them out.
This was the first time someone had ever given me advice in interpersonal communication, and after thinking it over, I decided that would be the smartest way to do it because it made sense.

Later when the rabbi came round, I was sitting on my bed in my room waiting for him to show up.

He came inside and sat down on the couch. He looked at me for a hard minute and then began to talk.

"I don't know you that well, and never had a chance to personally get to know you since you've gotten here. Things as you can see have been busy, and maybe that's why you felt you could take advantage of it.
Let's put aside what I saw you doing last night for a moment and let's talk about you. How is everything at home? "

I sat up straight as an arrow, and looked him dead in the face.
He struck a raw nerve. Whether he intended to or not, he caught me off guard.

I hesitated for what seemed like forever and managed to get out a one word answer.
"It's good". I replied.

"How is your father? He's a good man you know."

He looked at me very hard when he said that. As if he knew there was something to uncover and he was trying to figure out what it was.

This was a different type of exchange
This wasn't like any type of conversation I had ever had with any sort of yeshivah authority before.
His eyes looked at me with genuine care.
It seemed like he really wanted to know and wasn't just trying to make small talk.

All this time My father was still going in and out of the hospital, and still having one procedure after another.

Even though being far away from home was the strategy I had come up with in order to avoid confrontations and arguments with him, I was really worried about his health and missed my siblings a lot.

I felt safe and started opening up to him. I wasn't planning on letting him all the way in, but slowly as our conversation progressed I was struck by his genuine care and the way he assured me while I was talking with him.

First we spoke about my goals for the year and what I had come to the school wanting to achieve.

I explained to him that the reason why a lot of the feedback he heard from my past principals when he called them for references was negative, was because those people did not understand me and my speed of being able to grasp new concepts of learning. I told him how the past deans used to scream and ridicule me when they caught me learning other things, and that I really had a dream to finish studying all 38 volumes of the talmud.
Something that I was very close to achieving as I had only ten more volumes to go.

Then we spoke about my aspirations for the year and at this point I had gotten really comfortable with the flow of our conversation and started telling him more about what was going on at home and how my relationship was going with my father.

From the first day I was in yeshiva boarding school, it seemed that the best thing to do in order to keep the peace with my dad was to only call him once a week.

I missed my siblings and never really got the chance to talk to them either since in order to call them I had to use a calling card and there was only one phone for the entire dorm.

I used this as an opportunity to try and make him want to go easier on me, and told him that I just bought a cellphone on Friday and wanted to give it to him before it became an issue.
He ate this lie right up and I gave him a dummy phone I never used before, but kept for these exact situations. Since my father owned an electronics store growing up, he had lots of phones lying around and would bring them home for my younger siblings to play with. I took one of those and found a box for it, and always kept it close by. After what had happened last year I wasn't taking any chances.

He seemed surprised that I would just give him my phone, and after a few more minutes of talking, he brought up what he saw the night before in my room.

"Things like that can't happen again," he said.
After everything we spoke about tonight I have decided not to expel you and I won't talk to your father about this on the condition that nothing like this ever happens again.'

I readily agreed but he had more to say.

I appreciate the passion you have for learning and the dedication you show to your goals. I am going to talk with the dean this week about allowing you to build your own schedule, only if you can promise me it is going to help you intensify your learning production so you won't waste your time".

I started to cry.

This was the first time in a long time someone validated me without me giving them anything.
The first time in a long time that someone had shown me they actually cared about me and I didn't have to fight them first.
This was the first time I had felt like someone at the yeshivah actually gave a shit about my physical well being; usually they just berated me about my spiritual health.

I felt deeply that he was on my side, and decided to confide in him my deepest darkest secret.
Maybe he could get me help.

"I was sexually abused by my babysitter" I blurted out.

Dead silence.

He took a deep breath and put his hand on his beard.
He opened his mouth as if to say something, and closed it.
He sat there for a while with a pained expression on his face.
He was genuinely hurting for me.

"Wow, when did it get so late? He asked aloud with feigned bewilderment.

"I need to go home to my wife but let's talk about this tomorrow when I come back to yeshivah" He said, and got up to leave.

"Well at least I hadn't gotten expelled" I thought to myself.

He turned to leave and wished me good night. He reassured me that everything will be ok. I went to sleep that night feeling alot better than when I woke up that morning.
Someone else knew, and that someone really cared.

Chapter 17

I woke up the next morning very late and missed the first classes.

By the time I got to the study hall it was already afternoon.

I asked around and it seemed that the mashgiach hadn't been at school yet that day.
Where could he possibly be?
Is he trying to help me?
I allowed myself to wonder.

It felt really good waking up knowing that there was someone who knew my struggles and genuinely wanted to help me.

Evening period came, and in walked the rabbi.

He motioned me to come over to his desk and told me to meet him in his office after the evening prayers were over.

An anxious 2.5 hours passed, and I found myself sitting in a chain in his office opposite his desk.

He closed the door and sat down across his desk facing me.

I had never felt so safe in a school faculty members office before.

" I spoke with someone today who is an expert on addiction and recovery, and I think it would be a good idea for you to talk with him. He referred me over to a therapist who specializes in sexual abuse cases. Before you go I would like for you to talk to someone who has an organization to help victims get help, so you don't have to tell your parents you're going to therapy in order to pay for it. "

I sat there, and had no idea what to say.

This man was my angel.
This man took time out of his busy day teaching to make these phone calls for me and find out how I could get help.
Not only that, but he had also already spoken to the guy I was about to call in order to arrange financial help to cover this.

He looked at me with a kind smile.

"Whenever you are ready, let me know and I will connect you with them. "
I waited a moment, and then replied to him. I was ready.

More ready than I had ever been before to get this shit that's been plaguing me all of these years.

He dialed the number on his desk phone, waited until the dialer started ringing, handed me the phone and got up to leave the room.

I had never before had someone help me without asking anything in return, and I felt like I was rescued by a kind, caring lifeguard who pulled me out of the ocean right as I was drowning.

The call connected.

"Hello?" the voice said on the other line.
The name of the man who answered my call was E. He too, a survivor of sexual abuse.

We spoke for about two hours and as we wrapped up he told me this:
"You are a very brave man for being able to speak up about this. Most people wait until they are double your age or even later,to speak out and get help. You seem to have a lot of courage in you, and I have no doubt you will overcome this just as I did and change your life for the better.

You have a lot of strength to have endured all that you've

been through, and as you find the ways to work past it, you will see how this will all turn out for the better.
We are going to set up an appointment for you with one of our specialists to get help.
Don't worry about the cost right now. Focus on getting better."
I hung up the phone with a feeling of immense gratitude.

I felt like a weight was lifted off my shoulders.

Finding the words to tell the rabbi how I felt when he came back inside the office was hard, but the smile on my face through my tears told him I had a very good phone call.

I left his office with a renewed sense of hope and headed to sleep.

I stayed up most of the night researching the name of the therapist in order to read reviews about her, and all I saw was positive.

That night, I slept better than I had in a really long time.

The next morning the mashgiach called me over to his desk and told me he arranged a meeting for me with the dean for this afternoon.

He saw I was worried for a second, so he reminded me of what I told him that I wanted to learn more on my own. He told me to explain to the dean what I told him, and the dean would decide on what to do.
Ultimately, he had the final say.

Later that day, after talking with the dean of the school it was decided that I would start My rabbinic ordination in addition to the daily learning quota.

The only thing I had to do to keep the teachers happy was to complete the quote and get good grades on the tests. Not too hard.

The agreement we had came to give me time - almost 8 hours every day - to be free and do whatever I wanted so long as I was in the study hall.

--

Being that the school I was at was the last step in the system, they really only focused on two subjects: Hasidic teachings and learning of the talmud. (Chassidis and nigla)

There were separate teachers for both of them, and the way we learned hasidic scriptures and discourses was like this: we would spend the first hour or so of the lesson reading and learning the material on our own, or with a study partner. Then our teacher rabbi G would call us all into class where he would usually expound on one of the paragraphs at great lengths.

I was always more of a learn and move on type of student, and his classes felt like I was wasting my time talking about something no one ever fully understood, instead of trucking along and finishing the discourse. We'd sit in class for an hour, while the teacher would go on, seemingly lost in his own world of loftiness, his droning voice a nuisance in my ear.

I asked permission to stay out of his class and learn my Talmud instead. I was still in the top few of the class who'd get good grades on his tests.

I got it, and from then on, I would get up early every morning with excitement, and would usually spend my entire day either learning rabinnic ordination or the Talmud.

Talmud taught me how to analyze situations, and think critically.
Naively I thought it might do me some good in the real world I was about to face.

I also decided I was going to do it to make my father happy.

The next day, I started therapy with this therapist, and her outlook on life gave me a lot to think about.

To put things into perspective for you, until then, I hadn't so much as spoken to another woman other than my immediate family. I couldn't even look any of them in the eye.

I was frightened by them.

The trauma I was living with took over my mind and spirit, and I saw them as dangerous creators, who might hurt me at any time.
I was especially scared after they would do something nice for me or buy me a gift.
I would sort of wait for it to happen again but it never did.

Over time, It started to bother me that I felt that way since all they did was be nice to me and show me they care for me.
It was also one of the reasons why I was so excited to go to a woman therapist.

If I could overcome my fears and work through them all
the way and with a woman nonetheless, I'd be able to
heal myself from this fear forever.
That was my reasoning and that's what got me out of bed
that morning to make the one hour trip to her office.

Her office was far from the jewish area. I felt very calm
knowing that the chances of someone seeing me there
were a lot less.

From the first day I got to her office she saw how uneasy
I was and told me to choose any chair in the room to sit
on.

The way she spoke emanated an aura of calmness, and I
began to relax.
I spent an hour there and spilled out everything.

I told her the story of my abuser.
I told her the story of my flashbacks.
I told her how I was feeling affected by the trauma,
I let it all out and it felt so good.

I even told her I wasn't religious and I was struggling
with my relationships.

She just sat there and reassured me, and when my time
was up we scheduled again for two days time.

I had never had two appointments in one week.
Usually they were spaced out by 7-10 days.
I felt great knowing that I was going to be back soon and was in a really good mood when I left her office and headed back to school.

I felt like I was getting to the point where I would finally be able to work on this, and was starting to see the light at the end of the tunnel.

When I came back, I willingly told the mashgiach how it went.
He was happy for me, and told me he would let me leave in two days time, provided I would pass both my exams the following day.

I passed those exams.
The next day I was back on my way to Lori, My therapist's office.

That session she said we were going to work through my thoughts in order to figure out how to heal my flashbacks and panic attacks.

I left the office with homework.

I had to write down the problems I had with my relationships with people, and in a week when I would come back to her office I would have these two papers filled out.

I never found the time to fill them out, and the next week when I came to her office she was disappointed.
"If you aren't going to help yourself, who will then? I gave you this work in order to help you come back to me today prepared to talk about and come up with a plan on how to fix your relationships.
You have to put the work in however hard it might be and dig this up."

I spent the better half of our session just sitting in her office, staring at nothing.

I had been here for four hours already and didn't really feel like I was making headway anywhere.
My brain wanted actionable advice to work on fixing my own issues before I even wanted to hear about my relationships with others.

Either I did not do a good job explaining to her how I was feeling, or maybe this was the way traditional therapy was done, but I really wasn't feeling fulfilled with how this all was going.

When I was growing up, there was a lot of shame surrounded with going to therapy or having to turn to others for psychological help.

When it was spoken about, there were usually two sides to the discussion. The people who swore by it and the amazing things they have been able to overcome by it, and the people who were too scared to face their shit and denied that it was even possible to work out their issues while paying someone to listen to them talk.

People didn't just talk about therapy.
That left me to discover and navigate on my own how this all worked, and I had been doing so on and off for a few years now.
Spending money I did not necessarily have, in order to pay someone once a week to listen to me.

It was an interesting concept.

The more I thought about it the more I wondered if it was actually possible to develop myself on my own.

Without therapists or incompetent self centered rabbis.

I pulled out my phone and googled self help.

'Holy shit, I thought to myself. There was so much that

came up! Looks like so many other people had thought about this too and I was very excited.

I decided that going to Lori every week would be a great cover to get out and feel free for a few hours every week, so even though I stopped going to her, I still made it as if I had an appointment in order to get out.

I would take the train downtown and go for walks on the streets.

This really gave me time to listen to motivational speakers on youtube, and hear more and more about different ways to start making myself a better person today.

A lot of these things were stuff I was hearing about for the first time, and although I understood the concepts, I did not necessarily understand how to implement them. I would listen to these speeches again and again, and each time, I would feel like I was starting to understand.

Then there were days that I felt like I wasn't anywhere near where I wanted to be and that my whole idea was stupid.
I would finish the system just like anyone else and do what everyone else did. That was my destiny.

To do my best and try to fit into the square mold.
The problem was that I felt like a circle.
In order to fit into the square mold I would have to cut off parts of myself.

Something I felt I was doing every single day being in the yeshivah.

I would get depressed all the time and tell myself that I was helpless and I was never going to be able to be who I wanted to be.

I would spend my days learning, but over time my drive for that wore off and I always found an excuse to pop out of the study hall during sessions and would end up in the randomest places.

Sometimes I would go to the hotel, some days I would just sit in my room and use my phone, other times me and a few friends went up to the roof and smoked a few cigarettes.

The winter months in Montreal start in early November, and by the end of the month you couldn't go outside without a coat and gloves.

Chapter 18

There is one night I remember clearly in the middle of November 2014.

That night marked the beginning of the end of my time in yeshivah, and would catapult me into executing the idea of leaving for good, and speed up becoming a reality.

The night was a Hasidic holiday that was traditionally celebrated by a farbrengen - a hasidic gathering.
That night Rabbi G - my hasidic teacher was scheduled to lead the event.
I kind of liked Rabbi G for his personality and sincerity, so I decided I would sit down at the table and listen to him for a bit.
He had this droning type voice that soothed me into my own thoughts.

These were usually times of reflection, when everyone would come together and work on bettering themselves in their service to god.

When I was 13, The Spiritual advisor I had in Staten Island strongly encouraged us to devote a lot of time to prayers, especially on shabbat and special days. I used to take their advice with heed, and would spend most of the day in prayer, trying to connect myself to the source and get to the levels they said were attainable.

As I grew up, I had started to doubt everything they were talking about and decided that that form of devout service just wasn't for me.

In the beginning I was given a lot of talking to and rebuke that I was not on the level I should be, but after a while they just left it.

Suddenly I heard " …. And not like Brikman who thinks he's above all of this and does not have to learn from the chassidic teachings every day to keep him a God fearing person. You think I don't know you learn talmud before prayers?
What type of chassidic Bocher (youngster) learns written Torah before he has connected with his roots, with our teachers referring to the seven rabbis who were the leaders of the movement)?!

I tried to reply to this stinging attack, but before I could get the words out of my open mouth he continued lashing out at me. There was more for him to say.

" You think because I knew your grandfather, I'm going to turn a blind eye to what you are doing during my classes?

Quite the opposite!

BECAUSE I knew your grandfather I cannot stand by and watch while his grandson throws away the chassidic legacy he built.
If I told you about all those times your grandfather risked his life to keep to the tradition, maybe you would take this more seriously.

If Your grandfather and great grandfather were here today I'm sure they would feel the same way.
You ought to be embarrassed for the person you are becoming."

I felt my face go red.
My body got hot.
Sweat trickled down my spine.

"HE IS ATTACKING ME!"

My brain shrieked.

Before I had any chance to get a grip on myself, I felt like I had to reply:

"Who are you to tell me how to serve god? I answered back to him.

How dare you criticize me for what I learn - at least I'm learning! Focus on the kids who aren't doing anything at all and don't even know how to navigate your tests, I said in disgust.

The Room was silent in shock.
A Thick tension spread through.

Everyone knew that his farbrengen were always unusually sharp and harsh compared to the other leaders at the yeshivah, but honestly this was very out of line and really not like his character.
 I was done with it.
I got up and walked out.

Everything I was listening to about self development and growth validated my thoughts and feelings that how he had treated me was wrong and even abusive.

Definitely not like what I was used to enduring from other people in yeshiva but this hurt me on a whole new level.

I spent the night thinking and rethinking these thoughts to myself.

He had said I was an embarrassment to my family.
Is that how they really felt about me?
Who gave him the permission to say that?

Granted, he was supposed to be a spiritual leader and he was sharing with me how he felt, but it was shocking to me that even people like him could talk this way.

No one deserves to be spoken to like that.

If it really bothered him as much as he said it did, why hadn't he spoken to me all this time?
Why didn't he call me into his office to talk with me just like the other rabbis did?

Was his point to shame me in public?

I had grown immune to shame, and slowly, became immune to what other's opinions were of me.

On the countuary, anyone who even tried to offer any sort of unsolicited advice even if it was for my benefit and with good intention became the devil and I shut them out.

Both for the positive, and for the negative, I began to

shut out anything that other people would say to me that I thought was out to hurt me.

That night as I looked at myself in the mirror of my bathroom while brushing my teeth, I made a vow with myself.
I was going to keep on pushing on in this newfound pursuit of myself and who I really wanted to be, and won't give up no matter what.

Chapter 19

At this point, I felt like I understood how to communicate with myself, and so long as I was able to get my flashbacks and trauma under control there shouldn't be any reason I couldn't leave.

At this point I was halfway along my plan to move out and start over again on my own.

I was spending most of my non-learning time either drunk or on my phone. I also started reading the book -How to Win Friends and Influence People. I watched a lot of movies and tv shows. And the occasional porno.
I was still very uncomfortable with the whole idea, but masturbating was one of the very few things I still had that would make me feel good so I stuck it out every now and again when I was really bored.

My friend had told me a while ago that we could also use the computers at the hotel around the corner from our dorm.
Because I didn't really know anyone personally, I did not know that one of my classmates' parents owned it.
 Everyone went there for WiFi.

"That would be so much easier" I thought to myself. Instead of having to hide my phone all the time and read off a tiny screen, I could go use the computers and consume more content faster, without having to look over my shoulder the whole time because I was on my phone.

One night at about 12 am, I walked over to the hotel and started up a chat with the concierge guy.
He seemed like a really nice person, and after a while I figured he'd be a good person to ask my next questions.

In learning about living life on my own, I understood that I would have to support myself, and started learning all the details about how employment worked in the real world, and what a salary meant.

"How much do you get paid?" I asked him.
"Get paid?" I work for my money. He said. Looking at me amused.

"No, like how much money does work make you here? " I persisted.

"I get paid $22 an hour and after overtime I make $30." he said. Answering me more for entertainment because he was really amused by me.

What was a random yeshivah student doing at his hotel

at 12am?

What's overtime? I asked him.

He explained to me how the basic pay system worked for hourly salaried workers, and after he was done I asked him if I could use the computer.

"Only if you tell me your name". He said.

I got nervous. What, was he going to report me? Did he have some sort of deal with the mashgiach that he would tell him who came into the hotel and when?

I figured I don't have anything to lose.

My name is "Yossi," I said.
"Nice to meet you, Yosssi. Here is a paper with the username and password for the computer. He said as he pushed a paper with some wording into my hand. " Nice talking with you. "

The way he said my name made me smile, his friendly composure quickly making those thoughts of collaboration with yeshivah faculty dissipate.

I sat down in front of the computer and did not get up from in front of it till 6am.

I was able to google things incognito, and the more time I spent the faster a plan really started to take shape.

In the beginning, I would do this 1-2 times a week.
Over the next month, it became 2-3 times a week and then slowly every day I would be spending a big chunk of time sitting in front of the computer learning new things.

After all I had taught myself, I figured that all I would need in order to successfully start up on my own would be a job and a place to live.

I spent hours scouring job boards in states all across America looking for things that paid well.
I learned how to calculate the cost of living by state, and even learned how the US tax system worked.

The one commonality that there seemed to be, was that every job required a high school diploma or an equivalent.

Everything seemed to be a trade, which required previous knowledge, or experience, or some other sort of credentials.

Thanks to my strictly jewish education, I didn't even come close to having one of those or meeting any requirements.

There had to be another way.

I searched up how to get a job without a highschool diploma, and I read up on work that people do that was off the books. Someone posted in one of the forums I was reading that the best way to find work like that was to walk into a restaurant and ask to speak to the manager. Then, if they needed work they would offer you a job.

Seemed pretty straightforward to me, so I made that a step as part of my plan.

By the time it came early december, I was basically confident I knew everything I had to in order to get out of here and never come back.
It was around the same time, I started feeling a very strong pain and burning sensation in my right leg.

I tried to tough it out but what first was just a sensation became a ugly looking rash on my leg.

I tried not to give it any attention, and did my best to ignore it.

This has become a running theme in my life.

The house was on fire and it was filling the room with smoke. Instead of putting out the forest the source, I'd just run to another room.

Chapter 20

Because the yeshivah was in the middle of the community, every time there was a wedding in the community they usually invited the students.
There was a wedding going on one night, and my friend convinced me to come even though I wasn't feeling well.

I was telling him on and off what I was going through, and ever since that night last week we had the farbrengen, he was trying to do his best to cheer me up.

"I heard they have a full open bar there. Let's split a cab and go over. I'm sure it will be a great time, he said".

Maybe he was right. This would be good for me. I was in bed most of the day and this was a good chance to get out and drink away my problems.

I put on my shoes my hat and jacket and he ordered a taxi.

We spent the night chugging drink after drink and came back trashed out of our pants.

We would do this at almost every wedding. We went at every chance we had. It was the best way to get free alcohol.

We were usually so drunk by the time we were on our

way back, we always ended up having a DMC which would usually end with the consensus that we were right and everyone else was wrong.

It felt good to have someone agree with me.
So good, that I never took a second to stop and think if this was a good thing or a bad thing.

It was just another way to distract myself from reality.

That one wedding we went to I remember because I have a scar on my left third knuckle from it.
We knew one of the bartenders at the wedding from past events he'd worked at that we've been to, when he saw us he opened two fresh bottles of wine and just gave us glasses.

We did a few shots together and then me and my friend headed outside.

Somehow during our conversations I must have said something to piss my friend off, because next thing I know he was standing up over me, being very confrontational.

At that moment I was both so drunk and not really aware of what was going on, that when he threatened me as a

joke I got up and shoved him into a pole.
He in return dropped his bottle of wine and wine glass, and we began to scuffle.
Eventually we both ended up on the ground, and when I looked at my hand it was covered in blood.

"What the fuck man! " I scream out.
We both just stopped what we were doing and stared at my hand. Shards of glass had cut into my skin, and I was bleeding really bad.
To top it all off, my leg really started hurting again and I was barely able to take care of myself. I was so inebriated.

We both got into a cab back to yeshivah. No one spoke to each other on the way back, both lost in our own thoughts.

When we got back to school we both just went back to our rooms and went to sleep.

I didn't really like how this was becoming a regular thing and especially now since my leg was already in pain, Realizing my hand was swelling up did nothing to make me feel better.

The one thing I had to still figure out was where I was going to live.
A decision I really wanted some input on, but before I had a chance to deal with all of this, I was woken up one morning later that week by a much more intense pain shooting through my leg.
The rash had started oozing, and I couldn't put any weight on it.

I panicked.

I remembered how the dean in the last school I was at had issues in his legs because of his excessive drinking.

What would happen if that was the reason and the school found out I drank so much? What would my parents say?

Two days later, everyone at school was supposed to go home and spend some time with their families for Chanukah vacation. What will I tell my family when I come home?

These thoughts were interrupted by the Mashgiach rabbi W walking into my room. No one ever knocked when they came in, something that bothered me immensely since I felt like I had no personal space.

When he walked in and saw my leg, he started asking me a lot of questions. I tried to answer him as best as I could without getting anyone in trouble and in doing so he was able to tell I was avoiding him and avoiding some of his questions.

"We will deal with this when you come back, but for now, I need to take you to the hospital." He said.

I had a very big fear of hospitals, ever since my dad walked into one to start his chemo treatment.
It made him into a shell of the man he was.
Because I was so overridden with fears and phobias, this one too made its way into my head.
Had I taken a moment to think and rationalize that my father was very sick, and people who are sick bodies change as they are fighting their illness, at first I did not want to go.

Until the rabbi called my friend and we went together.

After a very long wait and multiple scans of my leg, and lots of questions of when I started feeling pain, I was diagnosed with Cellulitis in my leg, and had to come back for seven consecutive days to take an IV treatment.

Definitely not as bad as my anxiety had made it seem.

Firstly, I did not have to go home and face my parents because I was in treatment, and secondly because this was a very common infection that could have been spread by someone using the mikvah who had it.

I was off the hook.

On my third night of treatment, my friend, who had also stayed behind in the dorms and did not go see his parents, called me and told me we were invited to a Hhanukkah party the local chabad house was putting on.

I really was not in any shape to go, because now that I was in treatment and the meds started working I shouldn't be drinking.

The doctor had also given me strict instructions to keep my foot elevated and not walk on it if I did not have to.

My friend wouldn't hear of it, and one hour later we were in a cab, over to the event.

The rabbi who had invited us was very warm, and asked

us to stand at the door and ask everyone who was coming in, if they wanted to light the menorah.

I was in no shape to stand and wait, so my friend brought me a chair and stood next to me.

We spent the next hour or so doing just that.

After a while, we both got bored, and my friend went to find us both something to drink.
He came back a few minutes later with some food and a bottle of whiskey.
He sat down next to me and we started to be merry.

The alcohol helped me forget the pain I was in, and as it got later we got up to leave.
I don't know what possessed us to want to walk the 45 minute trek back to the dorms, given how I was feeling and the cold weather outside.

After about ten minutes of walking my leg gave out and I fell into the snow.

Both of us were drunk, my friend must have thought I was pranking him, because he started kicking me, nudging me to get up.

The pain was so strong that it started sobering me up. I tried to reason with him, and after a few minutes, we called a cab to take us back to the dorm.

The rest of the vacation was uneventful, and a few days later everyone was already back in the yeshivah.

I hid as much as I could about my life in yeshivah from my parents, and tried to give them as little information as possible about what I was diagnosed with and my treatments.

That's why, when the bill came for my hospital visit and my treatment, I had to pay it out of my own pocket.

All four thousand canadian dollars of it.

This expense cut the money I had to execute the plan I had into half. I spent the next day trying to come up with quick easy ways to make money so I would not have to forgo my plan to leave yeshivah.

After a few days, I figured the best way to make sure I won't get stuck would be to apply for a credit card.

I just turned 18, and asked one of the older boys how to apply for one, he sent me a referral link he had for one of the easy cards to get accepted for.

I filed it out and applied, and when I got my answer back I was delighted.

I was approved for a $2,500 credit line.

I had no understanding of what credit was at the time, and how it worked.
At the time, to me it seemed like it was free money I could use when I needed it, and I had to only repay a small amount of it till I had the money to pay it all. Until I could find work once I left to pay it off.

My hebrew birthday is the day after one of the most celebrated hasidic holidays, the 19th of kislev.

That year it came out on Thursday, so Wednesday, Thursday, and Friday nights were all celebrated with more farbrengen which led into shabbat.

That shabbat, the day of my birthday, we were all invited to the school Dean's house for a chassidic get together in honor of these holidays.

After Three days of drinking and celebrating and talking about self development in chassidic terms, they were making another one.

I was so over it.

When I turned 18 legally and applied for the credit card, this all started becoming very real to me. In honor of my 18th Hebrew birthday, which was ten days after my English one, I vowed to myself I will not drink another drop of alcohol until I figured my shit out and actually left.

I realized that I was using it as a distraction from the real world and the problems I faced, and on the day I turned 18 I felt a certain immaturity seep into me.

I was 18 now, and I had achieved ultimate freedom.
No one and nothing could tell me what to do anymore.

I decided to sit this one out and went to my room to take a nap. I planned to wake up after shabbat and go spend the night on the computer in the hotel.

Not a while after I fell asleep, my friend came in and woke me up.
He was looking for his drinking buddy at the rabbi's house and I was nowhere to be found.

When he tried to convince me to come, I informed him of my decision but he wouldn't hear of it.

He pulled me out of bed and cajoled me into my clothing. We set out for the rabbi's house.

When we came in everyone was there.

All the rabbis, even the one who lashed out at me last farbrengen of his I was at.

"Oooh look who is here! The Baal nigla (LIt. Master of the revealed torah) a demeaning terms used by chassidic teachers to criticize one who is too focused on the oral law and not on chassisim."

I looked at my friend who had brought me here and rolled my eyes. He smiled and told me to loosen up.
I felt like he might be in on this and tried to turn to leave.

He took hold of my arm firmly and we found a place to sit down.

Someone had mentioned it was my birthday, and this rabbi, who for some reason made me his personal attention case, started talking about the hasidic meanings of a birthday.

"Obviously the birthday boy isn't on the level he should be at spiritually for this birthday, but God willing next year with much work and dedication, once he sees the light of chassis for what it is, god willing things will be better."

Let's sing a niggun. (Hasidic melody) In the merit that his soul be elevated on his special day. Hopefully he will soon see that the teachings of our masters are important and he will start to follow their teachings. "

He started a melody, and everyone began singing.

I had no idea what the fuck this guys issue was with me, but every second I was sitting there was making me feel nauseaous.

I got up and went to the bathroom, and when I thought no one was looking I left and headed straight back to my dorm room.

I fell back asleep, and when shabbat went out I headed over to the hotel and picked up from where I had left off.

A few hours later, I received a frantic text message from my friend, telling me that everyone at the school was looking for me and I should come back right away.

I packed up and rushed back to the school in confusion.

I got back to the school and asked around what was happening. I was told the dean wanted to see me.

When I got to his office the dean's son in law, who was the administrator of the yeshivah, was sitting there, and motioned for me to sit down and shut the door.

He looked at me in a sort of gloating way, the way someone looks at you when they caught you red handed.

I had no idea what business I would have had with this school administrator, so late at night.

Matter of fact I never really even had said hello to him, until that one time I had to get something that was mailed to me from his office.

I found out that he had a close relationship with my dad, and I would randomly come into his office to catch up and say hello.

A talk with him this late at night was different than any other time we spoke, and the air had a sense of ominousness to it.

I was nervous.

He opened his mouth as if to start talking, and after what seemed like forever asked me " Yossi, do you know that stealing is a bad thing to do?"

My heart skipped a beat as I frantically started to think of what I had done that would be the cause of such a situation.

I had money, and haven't stolen anything for a very long time.

Besides that, he seemed to be a good person which is why I had trusted him in the first place. What could he possibly want from me?

"Yes". I replied back to him.

"Ok," he answered.

"Now we have two choices, you can either return the phone you stole today from the dean's wife, or I am going to search your room and make sure everyone knows it was you once I find it. " He said this in a threatening tone.

Honest to God I had no idea what he was talking about. I tried to appeal to him, but my words fell on deaf ears.

"Why did you leave early from the farbrengen today? Why didn't you wait until it was over to go back to your dorm room? Obviously you took the phone and ran back to your room to hide it. Be honest with me, you only have one chance."

I tried to explain to him what had happened and that I really wasn't feeling up to it in the first place but my friend asked me to come with him. I got up and left after I felt attacked and didn't feel comfortable being there. I literally had slept through the whole thing and if something was taken it was definitely me.

I knew better than to steal a phone that was able to be tracked on icloud. Not the year before that, that's exactly how I found my phone!

My explanation still fell on deaf ears.

He kept saying he was going to go to my room and search it.
I'm thankful for the lock that followed me through boarding schools that was on my door to prevent him from going in.

"I'm going to call the police," he said. I'm going to tell them you stole my mother in law's phone.
A last ditch effort in getting me to come clean. I had nothing to come clean about. I never took the phone.

Maybe he was trying to score points with his in-laws and he decided I would be his guinea pig, or maybe someone told him I wasn't shabbat observant so he thought it made sense.
I was so hurt and felt overwhelmed that he would think something like that about me.
Even when I did steal, I never stole from my friends or people I knew.

In my yeshivah days I only stole when I was desperate. It wasn't like a thing I did to pass the time.

Besides, I never saw him as someone who would threaten me, or wish me any wrong, why would he possibly do this

to me now, after we had built up this relationship together?!
Does everyone in the yeshivah feel this way?

I was too overwhelmed to think about it.

After he was done threatening me and left, I decided this was the final straw.

I had to get out of this place right away.

My usual choice when faced with fight or flight scenarios was to choose flight.
And this was no different.

I was done with being the kid everyone thought they could throw random punches at.
I was done with being the kid that was a prisoner to his own mind and kept failing.

I was done with living in fear of a system that had done nothing to me but cause me anguish.

I was ready to get out.

I took my new credit card to the hotel with me, and looked for flights for the morning. I found a cheap flight to Miami that was leaving at 5am, and began to make preparations for my departure the next morning.

I inquired about an Airbnb, and after some back and forth talk with the owner, the reservation was made.

The decision was made.

I was flying to Miami in the morning and had to take care of the final things I needed to do before I dipped out for good.

The first thing I did was call my parents, when my mom picked up, I asked to speak with my dad.
"Ta, " I said, my voice cracking a bit as I thought of what to say.
"I'm flying to Miami in the morning, I'm going to start my life again."

My father paused, took a deep breath and said " Yossi, I dont know whats going on with you right now, but I want you to know that Mommy and I love you and always only want the best for you. "

" I know that, " I said.

"I need to do this for myself. I'll call you sometime when I get there."

I hung up the phone and took a deep breath.

When I turned around, my friend was standing behind me.

He had heard every word I told my dad.

Chapter 21

My friend looked at me, perplexed.

"Who were you just talking to? " He asked me.
"My dad," I answered him.

You're flying to Miami in the morning? He asked.
"Yes," I answered him.
"I'm done here. I'm going to my room. Don't follow me."

I turned around to leave and went to my room and locked the door.

I started packing.

About an hour later there was a knock at my door.
It was Rabbi W. In his hand he was holding the phone I gave him not too long ago. He came back to school this late when my friend told him the news that I booked a flight to leave.

"Don't even try to convince me out of it. " I told him, all my systems were on high alert.

"I made my decision and I'm not changing it."
"I am leaving in three hours"

"I did not come here to try and convince you of anything, only to return what is yours. Go in peace and always remember if you ever choose to come back, our doors are always open. "

I always loved this rabbi for who he was, and hearing this from him made me feel like although it was going to be hard, this decision was the right one.
3 am came around and the taxi I ordered pulled up in front of the dorm.

My friend waited up with me, and helped me put my suitcases into the car.

He gave me a hug as I turned to get into the car.

"See you on the other side brother, good luck."

I looked at him and wordlessly got into the Taxi.

Here we go! On to the journey of a lifetime.

When I got to the airport with all my suitcases the airline wanted almost $800 to check them all in.
I decided to repack in the airport and left all of my other stuff at the airport lost and found.

I finally made it past security and got onto the plane.

As we taxid to the runway and the plane took off, this deep sense of calm mixed with deep sense of panic set over me.

I had done it! Successfully left the bubble I was raised in.

I slept through the entire flight, and woke up just as the flight attendant was finishing her announcement.

"Welcome To Miami!"

This all had brought me here.

I was sitting in front of the Ritz Carlton hotel in Miami with my backpack and my small carry-on.

Fuck, man. This was gonna be a rough one.

Chapter 22

I've fucked up in the past but This time shit was way more real than I ever thought it would get.
As it started getting dark, reality set in that I had nowhere to go. I had just under $500 left after I booked my trip and the apartment rental, and I had to figure out how to make that go as far as it could, but I also needed a hot shower and a bed.

I had not slept properly in over a day, and the exhaustion of the events over the last few days were taking its toll.
I took my bags and started walking up Collinsvenue, in Miami Beach.

I walked a few blocks, and as I was walking I was looking for a cheap place for the night.
I decided that I would book a room in a hotel, and shower and regain my bearings.

The gravity of what I had just done slowly began to sink in. This morning I was in yeshivah, and I just picked up on my own and booked a one way flight to a city I had never been to before alone.

I got to 21st Ave, and I saw a small hotel that looked cheap, and I figured if I had a chance at a deal, this was the place.

I walked inside and went over to the front desk.

"Hello sir, good evening. Staying here by yourself? A young guy, who looked about 25, came out from the back office and asked in a pleasant tone.

"Um, hi, yes, a room just for me please " I answered. I had never booked a hotel before, and had no idea how this worked.

"For how many nights?" he asked me.

How many nights can I get for $250? I asked him. I calculated that if I could stay here for a few days, I could spend the daylight going around to restaurants looking for work, and once I found a job I would figure it out.

"Well, it's $165 a night, which after taxes and fees comes out to $194.65. We have a special now, which is two nights for $349. Taxes and fees included. ".

I wasn't sure how to reply. $350 was more than two thirds of the money I had, and two days was too short of a time to be able to get my act together.

"Can I think about it?" I asked him.
He looked at me puzzled. "Sure," he said. "Ring the bell when you decide. You can sit outside at the pool and

figure things out if you need to before you check in."

"Thank you," I said and walked outside to the pool area which was facing the beach.

I sat down and pulled out my phone. After connecting to wifi and doing a few minutes of research, I realized just how naive I was. Prices for hotel rooms in this area were between $150 - $1000 a night. It became clear to me that had I not made this decision in such haste, I probably would have realized that and would not have sent my money to the guy I rented the apartment from.

This was a very important lesson I learnt early on, and it was the first of many life lessons I was going to learn over the next few weeks.

Lesson number one: If it seems too good to be true, it probably isn't.

There was another hotel about 20 miles away who's rates were almost $40 cheaper.

After calculating what it would cost me to uber there this late at night, I figured it would make the most sense to stay here for the night. At least when I woke up I would be close to all the beach stuff and would have a better chance of being able to find work in the morning.

There were a lot of restaurants all around - I was sure I'd be able to land something by the next day.
This sense of false positivity gave me a source of newfound energy.

I got up and walked back to the counter.

"Can I book for one night please?" I asked the same guy at the front desk.

"Are you sure?" he asked. Checkout is at 11 and right now it's almost 12 am.

Since I was really tight on money, I reiterated to him that I was only staying one night.

"Ok, " he said, " That will be $194.65. Credit card for the room and ID please."

I gave him my credit card and my passport.

He skimmed it over for a quick moment, and looked back at me with a scrutinizing look as if he was trying to figure out what my deal was.

He most likely saw my birthdate and was looking back and forth from my passport to me.

I did not have any other type of id, but that shouldn't be a problem right?

I was used to people thinking that I was way older than I actually was, because at 18 I had a full beard and looked like I was easily 25.

"Is everything ok? " I asked meekly.
" Yeah buddy, everything is alright" He replied back to me in a puzzled tone.
" There is a $150 hold that is going to be put on your credit card for incidentals. Your total comes out to $344.65. Sign on the screen here for me and then initial on the next page."

" Wait what? " I asked in alarm.
"You said it was $194.65 for the night. How is it $344.65? I only had $500 of available credit spendage on my card. If I was going to do this, I would be in the same scenario had I just gotten two nights.

This type of scarcity mindset had almost got the best of me, and in the end I booked the room for two nights and by the time I finally got up to my room it was just before 1am.

Breakfast started at six thirty, and I decided that I would wake up at 6, and get ready to spend the day looking for work.
Before I went to sleep I sent a message to one of my close childhood friends who I knew was in the yeshivah in Miami Beach. Which after some google maps searching, I realized was not too far away.

```
"Hey bro, I just landed in miami.
Message me when you see this, I need to
talk".
```

I took a shower and passed out.

I slept the sleep of the dead. Sleep was something I needed to catch up on, and when morning came and I finally rolled over, when I looked at my phone I realized to my dismay that I slept through my alarm.

"Fuck," I muttered to myself.
 Day one and I'm already losing.
I shot out of bed, and when I checked my phone, I had like 20 new messages and missed calls.

I didn't have service but whatsapp used wifi, since it was already almost 10:00, I rushed downstairs and tried to catch what was left of breakfast.

All that was left was fruit, rolls, and some butter, so I went to the front desk and asked if there was anything left.
To my dismay I found out that the hotel did not have their own kitchen, and that the food was delivered every morning. I was really pissed off because I was relying on breakfast in order to get my food for the day. In the end my estimated total was close to $500, and my card was almost maxed out.

I sat down in my room with a coffee and some rolls, and began to catch up on my messages.

The first one was from my friend.

"Hey Man, what brings you to miami?"

"Work," I lied to him. "I left yeshivah and am working here in Miami. Want to come by my hotel later and hang out?"

"Sure" He replied. " send me the address. If

it's close by I can meet you after the night seder. Let's be in touch.

" Great! Sounds like a plan." I replied to him. "Talk later".

The next text and missed call was from my uncle who lived in Miami beach.

"Hey Yossi, it's your uncle S. Your father gave me your number and told me you are in Miami. How are you? If you need anything please reach out!"

"Hey S," I replied. Thanks for your message. Everything is good! I came to Miami for work. I'm actually heading there now. Talk to you later!

The other texts were from my friends back at yeshivah and my parents. People I did not want to talk to so I ignored those messages and put my phone away.
I ate what I could and left the hotel. Headed in the same direction I came from, in search for work.

I walked into the first restaurant I saw, and asked if they were hiring.

The workers behind the counter looked at me puzzled, as if I was playing a practical joke on them.

I looked at my reflection in the store glass, and tried to understand what was funny, then I realized that they probably thought I was playing a joke on them because of how I was dressed.

All I had when I left yeshivah, were my white shirts and black pants. I was still wearing my yarmulke as well.

Picture a yeshivah student dressed in a white shirt and black pants, wearing a skullcap standing inside a Halal restaurant asking for work. I too would have laughed him out of my store.

Undefeated, I removed my yarmulke as I continued walking down the street, and nonetheless the same type of story repeated itself a few times in different restaurants.

There was one restaurant who took me seriously, and said that they were looking for a busboy for evening shifts. Even though the manager was there when I came, I was told they only do interviews for evening shifts between 4-8pm.

I was getting hungry and decided I would wait for 4pm to come so I could be interviewed for the job.
I walked outside, and tried to find somewhere cheap I could get some hot food to eat.

I settled for a pizza shop, and before I went inside I checked my credit card account. About $8.00 was all I had left, so I settled for a $5.00 sandwich.
I also ordered a pizza but in the business of the store and what was going on I never got charged for it.

I ate the pizza and saved half the sandwich for later. I did not know where my next meal would come from.
I walked around the shops and took it all in.

I didn't bother to keep looking elsewhere for work, because I figured that all I had to do was show up to the interview and I would have the job by morning.

That was usually how it worked when I wanted something in yeshivah. I was used to having things happen overnight.

Lesson number two: Always have options.

At ten minutes to four I headed back in the direction of the restaurant, and at four oclock sharp I walked inside and asked to speak to the manager.

I was here for the job interview.

Chapter 23

After about twenty minutes of waiting, some guy came up to me awkwardly standing in the doorway and told me to follow him back to his office.

He started off the interview asking me about my previous work experience.

I was honest with him from the start and told him that I just got here after being in school in Canada and was looking for work.

I had lots of experience with food prep and serving because for the two years I was in yeshivah in Staten Island I assisted with the responsibility of preparing breakfast and serving lunch and dinner to the school.

My father loved to cook, and I had a passion for cooking too.

"You do realize this is a busboy position, correct? He asked me.
"Yes," I said. I think I will do very well.

"OK", he said.

We will need a copy of your highschool diploma, and you would have to fill out an application for the position. We will send it out, and after we review all of the applications we will get in touch with you if we determine you are a good fit.

I sat there confused and asked aloud in wonder.
"I, I, I need a highschool diploma to be eligible for this job?"
"Yes," He answered me. It's pretty standard.

Well fuck me now I thought to myself. This was one thing they did not mention in those forums I was reading.

I did not have a highschool diploma nor did I have any sort of education that would come close to qualifying for a highschool diploma or GED equivalent.

Maybe if I had gotten my smicha certificate things would have been different, but it was too late now to ask the rabbi who tested me for that to send me the certificate. I was no longer in school and I did not even have a mailing address.

Realizing I would never qualify, I took the form he gave me and folded it up to put in my pocket.

"You sure you don't want to fill that out now and leave it here? I could use you on my staff as early as next week man. So long as your application comes back ok."

"It's alright," I said. "I'll come back and drop it off tomorrow. Thanks!"

I got up and walked out of the restaurant.
After walking away from the place and finding a wifi connection, I looked up "Jobs available without a highschool diploma" and the only thing that popped up in my search was craigslist.

From my past experience I knew that craigslist was kind of shady, and I really did not want to go that route if I did not have to.

I spent the next few hours walking around Ocean Drive trying to find for hire signs in the windows and randomly walking into places asking if they needed workers.

I was met with the same answer every time:
"We aren't hiring at this time. You can fill out the application online and if something becomes available they'll reach out to you. "

I walked back to my hotel room feeling defeated.

I had to check out the next morning, and I had no idea what I was going to do.
When I got back to my room and connected to wifi, a message popped up on my screen.

It was from my dad.

"Yossi, I hope you are ok and safe in Miami. We miss you and can't wait to hear from you. Call me."

I ignored the message, and instead texted my friend.

"Hey bro, I'm back at my hotel, want to come by soon?"

The time was now 7:45, and being that most yeshivas ran on the same schedule, which meant that by 9:30 he should be done with classes for the day and would be able to come see me.

This gave me just about two hours to come up with some sort of cover story or reason as to what I was doing in Miami.

It puzzles me to this day why I couldn't have just been straight up with him from the get go, because had I told him the truth, he probably would have been able to help me.

I took a shower, and when I got out I was happy to see a reply from him.

```
"Yo! School finishes at nine thirty and
your hotel is a 15 minute walk. I can be
there around 10. Is that good for you?"
```

"Perfect," I replied. See you soon!

I had come up with the perfect cover story. I was in Miami working for a guy who did sales online and was helping him get products. If he would ask me for more info I would tell him that I couldn't talk about it and be done with it.

At around 9:45 I got his text.

```
"I'm outside".
```

```
"Hang on one sec, be right down." I replied.
```

```
"Aight".
```

I went downstairs and he was waiting for me in the lobby. We said hello and exchanged pleasantries then we headed upstairs to my room.

"What's up bro! Long time no see! How's life, you left yeshivah for good?"

We spent the better part of the next few hours catching up.

I knew his family very well, and was avoiding as much of the real talk this conversation might lead to by asking about them and how they were doing.

His father was just in town for a visit, and he went on telling me about it. The mention of the word "Father" lined my face with disdain, and after another minute talking He looked up at me and saw the expression on my face.

"Everything ok?" He asked me.

"Yeah, I'm fine." I answered him.

A few hours later, we finished talking.

From what I had told him, it sounded like I had my shit together and I knew what my next moves were.

Honestly I don't know where I would be tomorrow, and the suriety I heard in my voice was so sincere, it even made me feel better.

I decided that no one would ever find out where I lived or what I did, in order to not stress myself out about keeping up appearances.

As my friend got up to leave he said " listen brother, it seems like you have your shit together but if you ever need any help hit me up".

I walked him downstairs and said goodbye.

When I walked back into my room and closed the door I broke down in heavy sobs.

I was hurting so much and I felt that if I put on a face that everything was ok then I might be able to change the reality I was in.

This worked for all of about one minute when I realized for the tenth time again today that the situation I was in sucked.

Lesson number three: Don't look back. You aren't going that way.

I could always go back, the yeshivah would welcome me with open arms and my parents would most definitely be delighted I was back.

Sitting on my bed playing with my phone, I kept pulling up my dad's message and the phone number the rabbi gave me to his personal cell.

This could all be over in a few minutes.

I would call them, told them I fucked up and then after a long few minutes of rebuke they would probably buy me a ticket back to yeshivah or maybe even home.

Home for me was not a good place to be at the moment, and going back to yeshivah was not something I was about to do either.

"Suck it up buttercup, it's always hard before it's easy." I chide myself.

I had no idea just how hard it was going to become.

I spent the night scouring job boards, and trying to find something that would give me hope for tomorrow.

Nothing.

I fell asleep with a heavy heart, and woke up the next morning to the phone in my room ringing loudly.

They were calling to remind me that I was a half hour late for checkout.

I got up quickly and took a shower. This would be the last shower I would take until I could find a new place to stay.

In reality I had so many places to go but for some reason no one could seem to understand I just wanted to be alone.

I packed my bags back up, and came downstairs with my bags. I asked the front desk if it would be ok to leave my stuff with them for the day while I went out.

They agreed and after I securely put my stuff in their office I set out again into the day to try and make something happen.

Lesson number four: When the going gets rough, keep fucking going.

Chapter 24

I walked back towards ocean drive, and stopped at every kiosk along the way looking for work.
I found an Israeli gift store that was selling gifts, and merchandise for beachgoers and walked inside.

I asked for the owner, and found out that he only came in after 4pm.

"What's with managers and owners always coming in so late?" I asked myself.

I could not afford to wait till then since I still needed to figure out where I was going to sleep that night.

I had always seen homeless people in movies, and even watched a few youtube videos on how to live life while being homeless.
I never thought this would become my reality and especially not like this.
Most of the videos I watched were stories of people who were once in a good place, and fell on hard times.
Only after they did not pay their bills for a few months did they find themselves on the streets.

Didn't people have to be something first in order to become homeless?

I was still processing what might very soon become my reality.

I would be lying if I said that I did not think really hard about making that phone call to my parents, and with every moment that went by, I wanted to just do that and be done with it.

"Get a Grip on yourself," I thought.

"You have been wanting to do this for as long as you can remember.
You need to show everyone that you can do this.
Remember all those people in school who always told you that you would never amount to much?

These people are watching your every move and want you to fail.
If you come home, they would have won.

Press onwards. "

Lesson number five: Other people's opinions don't matter if they aren't encouraging you to be better.

I always had the safety net of calling for help when I needed it.

Not that I used it much but it was very helpful when it came to good use.

Although the idea of not having to answer to anyone seemed really good in the beginning, now I sort of wished I had someone to answer to, who would take care of me and reassure me that things would work themselves out.

I walked down to 7th street, and saw a tent with a few homeless people sitting around it near the park.

Would this become my life?
Would I now live on the streets?
Would I ever be able to do anything in my life that wouldn't blow up in my face?

I had pretty much given up on the idea of ever being something the stories of success were made of.

I allowed myself to spend the rest of the day wallowing in self pity.
I let my depressive thoughts influence my decisions.
I hadn't eaten all day and my hunger jolted me out of my thoughts.

I really needed to figure this out and now.

I decided I would go back and get my stuff, and walk on the beach until I found a place to sleep. Then I will see what happens in the morning.

As I was walking back, my stomach started growling.

I walked into a restaurant and ordered some food.
I gave them my credit card to pay and when I swiped it one word came up on the screen: "**DECLINED**"

The server looked at me annoyed. There were people behind me on line and I was holding things up.
Frantically I tried to swipe my card again with the hopes that this time would be a different response.
It did not make sense to me. Yesterday I had $8.00 available and only used $5.00 for food.
What happened to my money?!

I sat down in the restaurant and pulled out my phone to connect to wifi and find out what was going on.

I pulled up my account and saw that I was overdrafted by almost $80.

The hotel charged me a $75 late checkout fee and that reflected on my account.

I was bummed.

No dinner tonight I guess.

I finished my walk back to the hotel and when I got there they handed me back my stuff and I went outside to the pool area to think.

A little while later one of the security guards came over to me and told me that I couldn't stay here any longer if I'm not a paying guest.
After trying to reason with him for a bit I realized that I had no choice but to leave.
I asked him for a few more minutes to finish up and he agreed.

I had no money.
I had no food.
I had no idea where I was going to sleep that night.

More than I wanted to admit it, I was scared.

I flung my backpack over my shoulder and walked out.

What does one do when they dont have money but need food?

I sat down near one of the many restaurants, and began to notice that a lot of people would get up before they fully finished their meal and leave it for the server to clear after they left.

After watching the same things happen with a few different people I decided the next person who did that I would go to their plate and finish their meal.

That's how I ate for the first week I was homeless, before I started getting recognized and chased away.

That night I found a spot close to south pointe beach. It was near some buildings, and close by I saw some other homeless people and walked towards them. As I got closer, I chose a spot near them with my eyes and scanned the area to see if there was anything dangerous around it.
I got closer and used my backpack as a pillow.
I laid down on the hard pavement and used my other hand to grasp the handle of my carryon, with the hopes that it would still be there in the morning.

The events of the last few days were all that was going through my mind.

I thought of my family.

How was my father doing?
How was my mom handling this?
How did my siblings react? Did my parents even tell them?

I thought of my friends at Yeshivah.

How did they react?
How did they tell them?
How did the person who took the phone from the rabbi's house feel now?

I thought of myself and how unfortunate I was.

Everything I ever tried to do in life never worked out.
Everything I ever tried to tell others fell mostly on deaf ears.
Everything I had invested into this was already gone.

All these questions were overwhelming me and keeping me from sleeping. I kept thinking about all different kinds of scenarios, none of which had a good ending in my head.

Come what may, I had already decided that there was no chance that I was going to reach out to my parents, or to anyone who knew me from my
"Past life" for that matter until I figured my shit out and came up with a way to get to the wealth and freedom I was always dreaming about in school.
I was going to start a "New life" and recreate the future, exactly the way I wished it to be.

I did not care that this was probably not a good idea. The need to prove and show these very same people that I was capable of doing what I wanted to, whether or not they approved of it.

They did not know where I was coming from.
They did not know the pain I felt.
They did not know the reasoning behind my decisions.

That was true, but honestly the only reason they never had these chances and never heard my story and did not know what I was dealing with on a daily basis, was because I did not know how to tell them.

Not that I had ever given them the chance to be privy to it or share this information with them.
That to me, was irrelevant.

I was mad at myself for how things were turning out.
I was mad at everyone for the abuse I faced.
I was mad at the world for all the shitty luck I kept having.

The more I thought about it, the more angry i got.

Usually when i had fucked up in the past, I would always point fingers and blame others for those things happening.
I would never take responsibility for anything that was wrong and I was the master at passing blame and skirting responsibility.

What made me so mad right now was that there was no one else left to blame but myself.

I had already wasted so much time these last few weeks blaming everyone for my problems.

The only person who fucked up here was me.

I did not, for the first time in my life that even knew any of these details to be able to shift my focus.

I had done myself in.

That night I finally realized what my dad had been trying

to tell me all those years and what we quarreled about a lot was true.

Lesson number six: Always own your shit. No matter how smelly it is. In order to be able to deal with an issue you are facing you always need to be honest with yourself.

Chapter 25

I must have fallen asleep close to the morning, and it wasn't before long that the beach cops were waking everyone up trying to clear out all of the homeless people for the beachgoers.

This was something they did every morning.
As the night would progress, more and more bodies would line the paths leading to the beach and some people would even sleep on the sand.
The cops would come around and sometimes even forcibly move people. The whole encampment moved up about 100 yards to the shop lined streets, where most of the people split up and went to their usual begging spots on street corners.

I walked around until I found a Starbucks, and went inside to use the restroom. I washed up and tried to plan my day.

I had no idea what I was going to do and had nowhere to be anyway so I decided I would walk back to the beach and hang out.

I sat there for most of the day, and just observed the passerby.

Sitting there for so long, and being the perceptive

inquisitive I was, I was picking up a lot of details from all the different things happening around me.

I noticed a guy walking around and pickpocketing people, while one of his friends distracted them by trying to hawk them his wares.

I saw the different vendors trying to sell their goods to passersby, and one in particular caught my eye.

You see, this guy wasn't like the rest of those sellers. This guy was in the sand, on the beach hawking his wares to people who were already settled who couldn't run away from him.

He really knew what he was doing.

I watched him for a while, and continued walking.

I saw lots of different things I had only seen before in movies, and was temporarily lost in the moment taking it all in.

I stopped along the way at the Ritz Carlton hotel, and admired all of the expensive cars parked out front. I was going to own one of those cars one day. I promised myself that when I get to where I want to be in life, I would own a black on black Rolls Royce phantom.

This dream, of course, was based on how I saw the world at the time.

To me, flashy cars, jewelry, and expensive houses were the signs of success.

Everywhere I looked I saw so many successful people driving around in their cars, and going out to eat with beautiful women seemingly enjoying their lives to the fullest.
That's what it looked like anyways.

I was jealous of those people.

They seemed to have everything set for them in life, and were always laughing with each other.
They guys seemed so happy to be with the girls, and the girls all seemed to enjoy the guys.

" Is it possible for me to have a relationship like that? I thought to myself. "After all that happened to me? "

I decided I was going to try it out.

But First, I needed to learn a trade out here to earn some money.

That night I came back to my spot later than I did the night before, and found someone else sleeping, in the exact same place I slept just the night before. He was drunk, and I did not want to fight, so I went to the beach and slept on the sand.

After a few days of the same thing; me walking around aimlessly doing nothing, sleeping in random places since this drunk had moved into my spot, one day I noticed that one of the cars in the junkyard near one of the buildings was not totally crushed.

I spent the rest of that day in starbucks charging my phone.

Throughout the day I would periodically look at my messages when I connected to wifi, and now I had some time to reply to them. Not like I was busy throughout the day, but that's what people did to appear busy.

That night I walked the length of the gate surrounding the junkyard, and found a hole in the fence I used to get inside. I walked towards the direction of the car, my adrenaline rushing through my veins. I walked as quietly as I could to the car which was sitting on the opposite side of the lot from where I got in and hoped no one would see me.

When I got to the car, to my joy, when I tried the door it popped right open.
I tried to sit down inside the driver's seat, and found that if I squished inside hard enough, I could get my entire body inside and slam the door closed.

After I buried my belongings under one of the junkpiles close by, I got back into the car and did my best to get comfortable.

"Welcome home," I snarked at myself.

I pulled my phone out of my pocket, and put some headphones in my ears. I turned up some music and leaned back in the seat trying to get some much needed sleep.
The metal bars of the seat kept digging into me, I kept adjusting myself until I finally felt comfortable.

At least I wasn't out in the open outdoors.

I was grateful for the fact that I had some sort of roof over my head. I did not have to worry about my belongings being stolen, and had some of the best sleep I had in awhile.

The next day when I woke up, I went to go watch the guy I had seen a few days before on the beach in the sand selling his wares. It took me some time to find him, because he usually only worked the beaches from the afternoon till night.

I found him working the pools that were near hotels. between the boardwalk and the beach.
There were some pools that had a fence around them, and there were others that were open making it easy to hawk his wares.

I watched him from a distance for some time, and was amazed how almost every single person he spoke to ended up giving him money in exchange for something he had on his tray.

As it started getting closer to evening, I saw him start walking away from all of the hotels towards a side street.

I followed him.

Partially because I was curious to where he was going, and partially because I wanted to have a chance to talk to him.

This man might be my opportunity to make some good money.

I could really use some of that right now.

"Excuse me?" I called out, while walking behind him.

He turned around startled and looked me up and down before answering.

"Que paso?" He answered in spanish.
"¿Cómo puedo ayudarte?"

I did not speak Spanish then - I was barely able to properly articulate myself in English.

"I don't want to bother you or cause any trouble," I said in English.
"I noticed you working over at the beach the last few days and I really wanted to know if you would be able to help me make some money. I see how you sell things to people and I really think I would be good at it"

"No, no. I don't know" He answered.

I don't know what it was that pushed me to keep talking to him, but I guess my problem of not knowing how to pass up an opportunity came in handy.

After a few minutes of trying to convince him I was serious he told me to meet him back here at 6 pm that day.

When the time came I saw him come into sight. He spent after a day walking along the beach and his box was empty.

When he noticed me, motioned me to follow him. We walked down a few blocks and turned into the driveway of a house.

We walked to the back and he knocked on the garage door.

Once we were let inside, I stood there for a minute and waited for my eyes to adjust to the light in the room.
It was pretty much dark, and smelled like cigarettes and weed.

There were two men sitting further inside, and the guy I had come with whose name I found out was Javier motioned me to follow him in.
We walked up to the men and Javier sat down with them.

It seemed they were all talking about me, and did so in spanish.

After a few minutes, Javier handed them some cash and got up and began to fill up his Box.

I had never seen it up close before since I'd always kept my distance, so now seeing for the first time what he put into his box was exciting.
This was some sort of stockroom, and he came here to stock up for his evening hustle.

There were cigarettes and cigars sitting in one corner, and they were stacked floor to ceiling,

There were also roses, trinkets of all different types, snacks, drinks, and alcohol.

He took eight cartons of assorted cigarettes, wrote something down and put them in his bag.
He then took about 30 cigars, and put them in his tray.
Then he added some trinkets, snacks, and drinks, and made sure to write everything down and then count it.

Once he was done, he motioned me to pick up the container filled with roses near the table, and we walked back to where the two guys were sitting.

I had no idea what Javier had told them just before but I was about to find out.
We both sat down facing the men and Javier handed them his list.

"Javier tells me you are interested in work" One of the men said in perfect english.

"Yes, I am. " I answered. "I am very good with people and can be very good at this". I said with false surety.

I managed to convince him and he explained to me how it worked.

Javier was responsible to pay them for these goods which he then sold wherever he was able to without getting stopped by the police.

They saw me as an unfortunate white boy who fell on hard times and needed help.
No one asked me where I came from because nobody cared.
I had, after all, only met them not even an hour ago.

They told me to spend tonight helping Javier, and every thing I sold myself they would pay me a small commission for.

Because I had no money they would use my commissions to pay for products, and instead of cash they would give me more things to sell and grow.

I did not really understand how it would all work in the beginning, but so long as they were telling me I would make money and get paid, I was happy.

I was feeling confident about this, and best of all, I did not have to spend any money in order to start working.

Not that I had any, anyways.

Chapter 26

We set off back in the direction we came from.
Javier loosened up and became friendly.

"You did well back there" he said, also in perfect English.

"Thanks, " I said, " but you didn't have to make It so hard," I joked.

We were going to get along very well, Javier and I.

This man taught me alot.

His family was of Cuban descent and he had been in Miami all his life.

Different from me though, he went home to his family every night.

The money he made went to help his parents and 2 siblings.
He has a very strong sense of family and as I got to know him more and more I became very impressed.

That's not why we were here though.

Javier was going to teach me how to sell. Something which seemed easier than it actually was.

Our first day, Javier took me along his usual route.
He was not used to other people watching him work so he told me to stand not too close to him and listen to what he was saying.

"Ok" He said, ``This is how it's done. "

"You walk over to someone who has a girl with him. You only walk over to the guys with girls. Then when you come over you say "Hello, roses for your girl?" And smile.

"Then what? I asked him.
"Come, I'll show you." He said.

I was intrigued, and couldn't wait to learn how it was done.
I followed him back to the beach and when we got there I stayed the distance he said to away from him. Just enough so that I could hear what he was saying.

He walked up to the first couple we saw on the sand, and smiled with a wave.

"Hola! Roses for your girl? " he said in more of an accent then he was talking to me just before. I figured it was part of his tactics.

"I'm good," The guy answered.

"What, you dont think she's worth it? " He shot back playfully.

"It's only $5. Do you want something to drink? Maybe water, coke, or beer? Tell me what you want, let's make a deal." I was amazed at how we kept the flow of conversation going even though the guy did not seem interested.

After about five minutes of back and forth the guy handed him a $20 bill.
He gave him $3 change and we continued walking.

"You see, " He said. "The customer has no idea that he's going to buy from me before I walk over to him. Once I walk over to him and start talking, I'm going to get the sale. I get it every time."

It was still early, and it was only later on that the tourists, vacationers, and people clubbing made it down to the beach and surrounding areas, so we walked for about a block before we saw another couple.

"You try, " He said.
"Me? I said in a half surprise, half panic.

"I only just saw you do this once, Why do you think I'll be good at it?

Lesson number seven: "You don't know if you never try amigo." He said.

This statement was so true to me that I got excited and we walked over to the next couple we saw, walking along the beach.

I eagerly walked up to them, and when I got close enough cleared my throat and said " Roses for your girl? " I smiled, and held out the repacked roses.

The guy looked at me and then at Javier and replied to me very nastily.

"You fucking people think you can come up in here and just walk up to whoever you you want and talk to them? I dont want no fucking roses get the fuck out of my face. "

I looked at Javier and he motioned me to keep walking.

I was shaken up from the ordeal and he saw that.

"You need to have tougher skin if you want to survive on the streets, man" He said.

Everyone here has got to eat. You're either going to eat or be eaten. You can't spend your time thinking about the nasty fuckers who won't help you eat because then you won't have enough to eat yourself man.

Lesson number eight: If their opinions don't pay your bills, they don't matter.

Chapter 27

I got my first sale after six tries.

I was watching this guy and girl get into it, obviously they were after a few drinks and some clubbing.

I walked over to them just as she finished going off on this guy, and just as i got close to him i said:
" Why dont you buy her a rose and some candy. I'm sure that will make her feel better. "
I was wondering to myself if this would work, and after a moment's hesitation as if thinking to himself and deciding it was a good idea, he looked at what I was offering him and pointed to two candy bars and a rose.

"How much?" He asked me. My heart fluttered with excitement.
"$12" I told him.
 He handed me the money, and I handed him his stuff.

I just made my first sale on the streets of Miami and it felt so good.

We did not have much time to celebrate - the night was still young and we needed to sell everything before Javier went home for the night.

I still did not know how his system worked with those people but we never had the chance to talk about it since we stayed busy.

I spent the rest of the night shadowing Javier all over the beach. Always listening to all his conversations and his witty comebacks. Most of which, after a few exchanges of words with those people he was talking to he got the sale. I was trying to figure out how he decided who to go over to, and what characteristics gave them away that they would buy.

I kept asking him questions and he would answer me sometimes and other times we'd just keep going. "You'll learn with time", he said reassuringly. You made one sale, no reason you can't make another.

I kept trying and after a while became desperate to try to make another sale.

Being desperate for anything is never a good thing and especially when you're trying to say something to someone else.

"Calm down bro" he said. It's all good just keep going. You're fine. You're doing very well.

At around 3:30 am, we sold out of everything we had taken from those guys' stock room.

Javier called it quits and told me he was done for the day. Before he headed home gave me $10 for my work and told me I did a good job today.

I didn't care that it was only $10 or that I still had no idea what this business was and if it was legal or not.
I was so happy to finally have some money and was looking forward to getting a hot meal.

We parted ways, and agreed we would meet again tomorrow.

I headed back towards my car and started to process the day and what had happened.

It dawned on me that I was so caught up in the moment, I did not confirm a time with him, or even a location to meet in the morning.

I started having a panic attack thinking that the one opportunity I had to make money came and I was too irresponsible to even get the details straight.

I kicked myself for this but slowly calmed down as I ordered food and sat down on the sidewalk to eat.

Tomorrow is another day and I should get some sleep.

I finished eating and walked to my car.
I checked to make sure my stuff was still where I left it the night before and was relieved when I saw they were.

I got into the car and tried my best to get comfortable.

I was excited for the morning to see where this new opportunity went.

Morning came and along with it came the Miami winter rain.

"Fuck", I thought to myself.
"No one's going to be on the beach today. "

I spent $7 on dinner last night and had $2 in bills and some coins.
I learned my first lesson in budgeting.

Lesson number eight: spend less than you make.

I did not know if Javier would be on the beach today since it was raining, so after about two hours in Starbucks reading missed messages from my dad, ignoring other people who wanted updates, I walked up the beach and then turned towards the house we went to yesterday.

I figured if he wasn't there, at least maybe I'll have a chance to talk to those other guys and find out more of what's going on here.

As I was walking along the way I saw Javier coming from that direction.

"Hey man sorry I left you like that last night" he said. Come let's sit down and talk.

Chapter 28

We walked a few blocks to a Cuban coffee shop that I literally never would have walked inside of had he not told me to come in with him.

We sat down and he ordered coffee and a sandwich.

"Do you want anything?" He asked me.

I looked at the menu, and checked the pricing. With my $2 I barely had enough for a coffee.

"I don't have any money bro" I answered him.
"Can't order anything". He laughed and said "breakfast is on me man. Nice work yesterday. I have never seen someone pick up quite as fast as you did."

When I declined - I was never used to accepting things like that from people he laughed and said:" bro, You made me $30 yesterday. Eat up. We have work to do. "

As we sat and ate, he started to explain to me how this business all worked.

The people we saw at the house have an agreement with all these types of beach sellers, and everyone comes to them at their specific time during the day.

Because of how well they knew him, each item he chose to take is written down on credit, and at the end of every night he must pay them.

They have his address, phone number and family info.

Over time, they let him take more and more stuff on credit and he pays them once a week.

One time he made almost 25,000 in two weeks.

My eyes lit up at the mention of such money. That was enough money for me to live for an entire year, I thought to myself. I was even more enthusiastic to get really good at this and make the money I always dreamt about.

"How do I get to do the sales like you do? " I eagerly asked him.
"I want to make money like that to be able to support myself and move into a real apartment like a normal person. I sleep in a car now man"

I was beginning to become desperate to get out and into a better living situation, and it was really distracting me from focusing on anything else.

Homelessness, changes your entire perspective on everything.

For me, I went from sleeping in a comfortable house, and later on a dorm room with two pillows in my bed every night, and air conditioning when it was hot and heating when it was cold.

Here, when just trying to make it through the day, and eat whatever I could find to stop my stomach from growling became my daily struggle. Things like where I was sleeping and how I looked and smelled became second priority.

I was grateful for the showers on the beaches and the soap people would leave behind. After I found a forgotten towel on the beach a few days in, I was able to take a shower whenever I wanted and it wasn't so bad.

I was going through so many transitions at once, that I wasn't always focused on what I came here to do in the first place.

Matter of fact I wasn't even sure what I was doing here anymore.

"Look man, " Javier's voice jerked me out of my thoughts.

"The way I see it is that you have a very big potential to get very good at this.

You watch me for a few more days, and after I feel you are ready I will give you some things from my personal items to sell and we'll see how you do on your own.

After that works out we'll figure out a way to get you accepted and sell on your own."

So far in these last three days I had learned a few very important business lessons, and I was excited to keep learning more.

I found a new obsession in chasing the highs closing sales gave me.
Every single time no matter how much the dollar amount was, I felt so proud of myself for being able to convince someone to spend money with me.

The rest of the week went on and like clockwork, every day at 11 am we would meet on the beach and get to work.

By the end of my first week Javier handed me $300 and told me this was my profit.

6 days and I made $300. It wasn't much, but it was enough for me to buy some new clothing.
Till this time I was still wearing my white shirt and black pants, together with my black sneakers.

I bought shorts, a shirt, sunglasses, a baseball cap and even got a haircut.
I hesitated when the Barber tried to cut my beard, but after him reassuring me it would come out nice I agreed.

After all that, I had $200 left.

Because I did not want a repeat of the sinking feeling I had when I only had $2 for food, I saved $100 for myself and told Javier I wanted to use that money to buy some items to sell on my own.

He gave me ten packs of cigarettes and five roses, and we agreed to meet back at our spot at 5pm.

I was out on my own for the first time and had an opportunity to make $50 in just a few hours.

I set out in the direction of the spot he tried to work with a bounce in my step.

I had made it.

I was finally going to make some money and start to figure my way out of the shit pit I fell into.

Things were looking up.

Chapter 29

With every passing hour my excitement started fizzling out.

I walked the beach like usual and the areas we usually went to weren't full at all.

The weather wasn't great and the few people who were on the beach weren't interested in talking to me at all, let alone buying anything.

That familiar feeling of defeat and doom started creeping back into my head and I reminded myself what kind of failure I was and that doing this was a stupid idea and I never should have tried it to begin with.

Depression is such a scary thing because you never know when it might hit you.

I needed a drink.

I don't know why I hadn't thought of it sooner, because after thinking about it a drink was the perfect solution to my problem right now.

"No," I told myself.
"You aren't going to drink now. "

I hesitated for a good few minutes in front of a bar and realized that I couldn't even buy alcohol because the legal age was 21, and a beer was $9 and served in pints.

"Screw that. " I said and sat down in front of a Starbucks to connect to WiFi. I opened up my YouTube and came across "The strangest Secret in the World" , a book by Earl Nightingale.
I listened to the whole thing in one go and then pressed replay and listened again.

I strongly encourage you to listen to it.

I don't know what it was that suddenly hit me but I felt like I was given a new perspective on everything I was going through.

The realization that I was actually in control of who I wanted to be and that I was in control of the outcome because of the thoughts I allowed myself to have was very powerful.

The only thing missing was my own action.

5pm came and I managed to sell one box of smokes.

I came back to the meeting point feeling shitty about myself, and I decided when we were done that I was just going to go to the beach and look at the water.

I had a lot of thinking to do.

It seemed to me like everything I ever tried to do was met with some sort of pushback that made it harder to accomplish than how it seemed when I thought about it in my head.

It seemed so clear to me how to do this before I started out, why did it become so much harder?

Why couldn't I just do things like everyone else?
Why couldn't my life be as simple as everyone else around me seemed to be.
Why do I have to go through all this pain?

I thought about my family and my dad.
I thought about my friends and the people I knew.
I thought about the way I saw my future becoming and realized that sales would be the way I was going to do it.

I just had to get good at it.

I realized that every no brought me closer to a yes, and that changed the game for me.

I spent the next few days really busting my ass to get in front of as many people as possible.

Chapter 30

Most people don't realize that homeless people usually had a life before they took to the streets.
Taking to the streets and living on the edge might seem like a good idea when it seems to be your only option but it's really not ideal and I do not recommend it.

Most of the people I met on the streets usually had a few things in common:

1. They never took responsibility for their actions. There was someone else to blame.
2. They would not take ownership of their faults, even if they were logically shown they were so.
3. They were very resentful and hateful towards the world. I was too.

But I knew there was something better.

All those people who walked around the beach every day proved to me there had to be.

There was this guy who usually spent his nights posted up at the entrance to the beach, begging passersby for handouts.
It never occured to me to do that since I had zero trust for other people, and when I learned how sales worked I felt I found my calling.

When I first started making money with Javier, I eagerly tried to offer this guy a job so he could make money and move on with his life.

He was a bit older than me, and I really felt like if he got into it he could make it work.

Whenever I tried to talk to him he would just wave me off and was not interested.

"You only live once man" he would always answer me. "I blew my chance. Back when things were good I'd never be here man. It's like one day I was on top of the world and the next day I was out here begging for money.

If I had something better going for me, I lost it on my way down. No one cares about me and I'll just be here till I die.

Why would he choose to be complacent with this reality instead of trying to change it?

It didn't make sense to me.

After repeatedly asking him and getting the same answer, I realized there are two ways to look at your problems in life.

1. You can either choose to face your problems head on, and take ownership of the outcome you want to create.

    OR

2. You could play victim to your circumstances and live a life of pain and hardships caused by your own laziness.

True, you only die once.

But some people never really live.

I decided I was going to live.
I was hiding from All The pain and suffering, and I knew that some day or another I would have to face it head on and make something of myself.

This was not a way to live.

I would not prove everybody right and be another statistic.

Over the next few weeks I amassed enough money to cover rent on an apartment, or so I had thought.

When I went to check out the place I learned that the traditional lease usually needs three times the amount of the rent to move in.

 First month's rent, last month's rent, and the security deposit.

I was pissed because I was growing tired living with this reality and had to make some changes
I was done with living on the streets. I had to figure a way out.

Then one night there was a fight I watched where two homeless people fought each other over a place to sleep. Two grown men. Fighting over a square on the pavement. This to me, was rock bottom.

I got up and started pacing the beach.

I desperately needed help.

I needed to get away from this mess and start over.

But..... How?

I knew I had family in Miami Beach.

The thought crept in to the back of my mind:

"Maybe, Just maybe i can call them and they will help me?
Can i trust them,? "

As the day wore on and the night started moving in, I braced myself and thought hard.

I decided I would call my uncle, and in a few words told him what I was up to and where I was.

I decided with myself that there was no shame in getting help.

I was born to make mistakes, not fake perfection.

So long as I would learn how to process those mistakes and learn from them in the things I chose to do in the future, mistakes are small learning experiences that shape the future.

20 minutes later his minivan pulled up and he took me to his parents house, where they prepared a room for me and graciously welcomed me into their home.

Smelly clothes and all.

I decided that I was going to try and find some work in the Jewish community.

I was about to begin the next chapter of my life.

Besides getting good at sales, I also had to learn how to get good with money.

This was one of the main things that influenced my decision to reach out, even though it went against everything I had stood for in the beginning.

Since renting an apartment would cost me money I did not have and I was already in some debt, having a place to crash at his family and later at my cousins house was something I'm very grateful for.

Once my uncle picked me up my dad found out I was doing ok.

He sent me a number to one of his friends and he connected me with someone looking for a sales guy.

If my father was willing to put his name on the line to help me find a job, I was confident that I would do well if I gave it my all.

My cousin was gracious enough to drive me and this began a new chapter.

The old me was put to rest, and the new me was reborn.

I realized over the last few weeks that even though I can't control where I came from, I am totally in control of where I was going.

This realization helped me put my differences aside and man up to even being open to my father's help.

The drive to the office was silent.
We were both deep in thought.

We got to the office and she pulled up to the parking lot.

I took off my seatbelt and clicked open the door.

"Good luck! " She said, as I stepped out of the car.

" Thanks! I'm gonna need it. "

This was my new beginning.

The Job turned out to be exactly what I needed for my first few months alone, and I am grateful for that experience.

I still had a lot to learn, but I was on a good path.

Part 3:

Money Matters.

I wish I knew more about how to manage my finances when I first started life on my own.
Here is the simple breakdown of what I learned.

Chapter 31

I can add another 250 pages detailing my life over the course of the following years.

But that's not what you're here for.

You are here for the fix to your broken, and over the next few chapters I am going to lay out different Mini work books with simple easy to get started steps that I have used to overcome the struggles I have faced.

I did not know this at the time, but looking back at the fact that someone was willing to stop what they were doing to come pick me up, and take care of me did more good for me then I ever thought it would.

This was the first time I not only accepted, but was actually grateful for someone else's help, experience, and guidance.

Not that anyone I knew was prepared for what I was going through but the mere fact that I now understood how hard it can be in "The Real world" Humbled me out and forced upon me a reality check.

Over the last five years in business, I've learned my way around industries like electronics, real estate invesments, sex Toys, mortgage loans, self development, online sales, social media marketing and business development, until I got licensed as a Realtor.

I have only worked one job with a paid salary.

After that I was on a commission only payment structure and still am to this very day.

Looking back I wish that one of the things I had learnt before I left the Yeshiva system was how to manage money, how different forms of employment worked and how the government collects taxes.

If you are reading this book, and it is your first time hearing about how the workforce works, I'm going to explain it briefly here.

Let me be clear that I am no business coach and do not have any science or statistics to back this up other than my own, but if you read this until the end and employ the strategies I've shared you will definitely learn something.

I only am going to talk about my experiences and the things I know for a fact because I've done them.

I Never learned about basic employment and how it works. To make up for that, especially if you are using this book as your battle plan, here is a quick simple breakdown you can understand:

The Workforce:

The most common form of employment in the United States is a salary paid by the hour.

The average person works a 44 hour work week.

That's 176 hours per month, or 2,112 hours per year.

The Minimum wage as of the writing of this book in Florida is $7.25 an hour or about $16,000 A year.

The process to get a job in the workforce is fairly simple:

You look for a business near you that is hiring.
You go and apply.

You get the job and start trading your time for money every day until you die or retire.

Over the first few weeks you get trained, and then you know how to do whatever the business does.

Over the course of time you try to get better at it in order to get promoted, and be more recognizable in the company.

This works for most people, because the general public that goes through school and college, learns how to become good workers for other peoples companies.

Nothing bad about that, afterall, they have been learning how to become good workers since the first day of school.

We are taught, do a good job and you will be rewarded. Don't do your job well, and no one will want to work with you.

It became clear to me when I started my first company and had to hire people to work for me.

When I typically hire employees I look at two factors in determining their value.

The first one is work ethic, the second is whether or not they can be a team player.

If they met those requirements, usually they would get the job.

As the saying goes, You can't teach skills in one day, but you can teach skills to someone who never gives up.

It's pretty simple and straightforward.

70% of The workforce in the United states makes their paycheck this way.
 3 out of 5 People working this way are living paycheck to paycheck.
The second type of Employment is those who are Self Employed.

Independent contractors, Commission based sales Representatives, Entrepreneurs, Dream Chasers.

People who have bigger dreams than just getting by, and who want to Maximize their potential choose this path because of its unlimited income benefits and the freedom it provides.

Chances are, most of the modern day successful people you look up to are self employed.

Being employed in such a way requires a lot more discipline then the average worker, since you are the creator of your own schedule.

Working this way means Your income is directly affected by your productivity, which is both a good thing and a nerve racking concept all in one.

One the one hand, the more concentrated effort you put into learning your industry, and constantly striving to be the best pays off, eventually.

On the other hand as human beings we sometimes tend to get distracted, and are easily put off by things we are uncomfortable with.

It's very easy to have an elaborate plan of how you are going to conquer the day when you wake up at 5am.
The first few hours go well because no one else is up to distract you.

Next thing you know, something happens, and before you know it you've lost an entire day of productivity due to unforeseen circumstances.

These are the troubles of people who lack discipline and don't really understand the basis of time management.

As I set my sights on more goals I wanted to achieve, and things I wanted to accomplish, I realized I would be better off. If this is you, keep reading.

In order to be able to align with people who match this description, I realized that I needed to work on these traits and always be perfecting them.

When I first got into sales and tried to figure out my worth I discovered a few things about the value of money and how people use it.

Money for some is a commodity, by which use of it acquires new things.
Money for others is a vile enemy who controls them.

The difference is in the way you govern your mindset.

I found this simple acronym to have been a major help, and I added my own personal touch.

W.E.A.L.T.H

1) Write down what you want.

2) Envision your future.

3) Affirm your desire.

4) Assume ownership.

5) Listen to your inner voice.

6) Take action and transform.

7) Hold the vision and don't give up.

W - Write down what you want:

Every Successful person I know has a list of wants and visions, just as much as they have a list with clear goals and actions they must take in order to achieve those goals. How to set a goal is fairly simple:

1) Decide. Think of something you want to do or work towards. It does not matter what it is, so long as it's something you want or are interested in. Something you want to achieve for yourself. (E.g. A million dollar sales volume, a happier wife, lose weight, Etc) - It also helps if your goal seems a bit out of reach. Nothing good ever came from living in your comfort zone!

2) Now, Write it down.

E - Envision your future.

3) Take a moment to Close your eyes and envision what the outcome of the goals you have just written down would be. Allow yourself to get excited for the possibility of change, and invite new energy into your life.

How awesome would that be?
How amazing would it make you feel knowing you can accomplish anything you set your mind to!

A - Affirm your desires

4) Tell someone you know will be a source of unwavering support throughout your new journey. Try not to tell people you know will have something negative to say.

You don't go through this alone, but you also want to protect and soundproof your mind from any negativity.

A - Assume ownership.

I added another "A" to emphasize the importance of assuming ownership and making this goal yours and not just a dream.

> 5) The most important step before you take action is to own your goal by breaking it down into human sized accomplishable feats. Especially when you are talking about a big long term goal.
>
> Once you have a big goal you want to accomplish, set lots of Mini-Goals along the way to make it easier for you to accomplish them.
>
> For example, When I lost weight, I knew that I wanted to lose 50 pounds, but I broke it down into 5-7 pounds a month. That helped me see this goal as manageable, and ultimately made it easier to stay focused and obtain.

This helps, because over the course of time, you accomplish many Mini- Goals which build your self confidence.

6) Lastly, Plan your first step.

If you don't plan it, frankly, you will never start.
Ultimately, the only way to get started, is to actually begin.
 You want to make sure you have a thorough plan that you will commit to stick to.

There is never the perfect moment to begin.
You are the one in control of when you decide to begin your future.

The first step is most important, because it sets the tone for how the rest of your trek is going to go.

L - Listen to your inner voice.

7) Throughout the process of achieving your goal, You will be met with lots of obstacles in your way that you will have to overcome. It's important to spend time with yourself reflecting and affirming the capabilities you have to achieve them, and arm your mind for when they are challenged.

If your goal is big enough you will find yourself constantly in doubt if what you are doing is even the right thing and that's where being grounded and well planned out can really be the difference between success and failure.

Personally, I find daily introspection and meditation helps me stay focused and calm no matter what challenges come up throughout the day.

T - Take action and transform.

8) Even the best plans are worth nothing without action. That first step is only as good as the one that follows it.

No matter how good a system and process you have come up with to achieve and win, it is worthless if you do not put it to work.
Even after you do start working, the path to greatness and achievement is filled with every sort of reason and excuse for those seeking an easy way out.

I call these Character Testers which ultimately force you to grow and become better.

Along this process you are going to be forced to confront yourself for who you are, and dig deep to bring the change you want to see.
The more you work on yourself to accomplish and stick to your goals, the stronger your character becomes.

Countless people have created the grandest ideas, planned the biggest goals, and talked about the massive success they planned to achieve - but gave up at the first roadblock.
Along the process you will be met with lots of these people who have given up on dreams and goals of their own. It is important to not pay these people much heed, and do not listen to anything they tell you.

Words mean nothing, when actions show the complete opposite. Don't you agree?

It is so important to Keep Your Focus clear and repeat the actions you've committed yourself to daily, in order to see and achieve your goal to the end.

The more persistent you are in seeing your accomplishments through, the more of an impact you will make. Both on yourself and on the people around you.

If you ever feel like you need more mind food to stay focused, think about all the people in your life who are relying on you to succeed. How would you achieve your goal to make life better for the people in your life?

If you're trying to lose weight, think about how much better life would be with your spouse if you had better stamina.

If you're trying to overcome and beat a habit or addiction, think about how much better you are now that you are more present for the people in your life.

If you're trying to make more money, think about the betterlife you would be able to provide to those you love when you accomplish those goals.

You get my drift.

I take my responsibility to my goals seriously, because I know how important my results are to the people around me.

Remember this: A river cuts through rock not because of its strength, but because of its persistence

H - Hold this vision and don't give up.

9) Giving up is not an option, right?

Once you've taken action and started the journey to your goal, the first few days will be bliss and you'll be enjoying the adrenaline rush of "New Beginnings".

After a few days reality will slowly set in, and you'll be asking yourself if this is all really worth it.

There are a few things to prepare for whenever you start out to achieve a new accomplishment that I have used to help keep my focus clear and not give up when the going got rough.

Working towards my goals sometimes felt difficult and frustrating, but I still needed to persevere.
When I was struggling, I learned to ask other people I know who have been through similar advice, and ideas for what else I could do. Sometimes hearing things from a different perspective gave me new ideas on what I could do.

Thinking about different ways of reaching your goals makes it more likely we'll be successful.

When I really felt stuck, I took a break, cleared my head, and then re-read the goal I wrote down when I first started.

It's ok to adjust your goal.
So long as you are constantly planning and executing your next steps.

    10) Things might have to change, but remember: slow processes are better than none.

This is where it is very important to "Remember your why" and the reason you decided to start all of this to begin with.

A "WHY" Is the reason for why you are doing what you are doing to begin with.

Your Why is your motivating force and it's important to always be conscious of it.

Whenever I was faced with a doubt whether to do something or not, I would refer back to my why and ask myself:

"Is this bringing me closer to, or farther away from my goals?"

The answer to that question alone, when answered truthfully is the easiest way to stay focused.

If it was bringing me to my goal, I'd do it to the fullest. It if was farthing me away from my goal, I would avoid it like the devil.

There is nothing that can stand in the way of your will.

Plus, I had a lot of motherfuckers to prove wrong.

Chapter 32

When you work, you make money.

Most people use the money they make to pay for basic living expenses, like food, a house, a car, etc.

Growing up, I am grateful that I never had to worry about it.

As I grew up though, I began to realize that money was something that was seldom spoken about, and financial literacy was something I had to learn on my own.

I am going to explain this concept briefly here:

There are a few key reasons why people want money.

Firstly, people will pay money to feel good about themselves.
The more money you have, the more you can feel good about yourself. Right?

Secondly, look at all the things money can aquire!

People will pay good money for something they find valuable.

Cars, planes, boats, houses, and expensive toys are all worth the money they are worth because people find them valuable.
People find them valuable because having things like these make you feel good about yourself.

Or distract you from the pain.

To some, Money is an illusion of power.
To others, Money is a yardstick to measure the service they are providing to the world.
It is very important to remember that no amount of money can substitute, or make up for lack of character.

Lots of people start off in their journey looking for the quickest way to make money in order to feel good about themselves.

There is a reason why "Get Rich Quick" Schemes are still alive even though most people know that these are fake, and just schemes to make a dishonest buck.

The truth is, there will always be those people who are not willing to put in the work required to earn their pay, and take advantage of the less informed for a few dollars.

Instead of using their skills to make larger amounts of honest money, these people prefer to prey on those who are dumb enough to think that wealth can be amassed overnight.

These days we live in a world where people will sell the shirt off their back in order to "Keep up with the Joneses" and have that nice new car, flashy house, and model family.

It's easier to get sucked into that crap and lose focus of what's important.

I love to use an example from the movie classic " The Italian Job".

(If you haven't watched the movie I recommend you watch it. After reading this book it'll give you lots of really cool insights into the human character.)

After they completed the heist of the safe from the house, the scene opens up with all of the team standing on a cliff, talking about what they are going to do with the money they just made.

Each character goes through with excitement talking about what they are going to get,

when it comes to Steve's turn he says

"You know, I am going to get one of each of the things that you just said."

They all laugh at him as if he is silly. Little did they know he planned the heist that will kill John Bridger, and make off with all the gold.

The movie goes on to show how they track him down and make a plan to take him down and get the money back.

He literally went and bought one of everything that everyone said they were going to buy.
He did not have any backbone of his own and was just trying to live other people's dreams.

The only way they were able to track him down was because each person on the team had invested so much time into planning all of the things they wanted to get, that they knew exactly what his next move was.

He was predictable, and that was his downfall.

I love using this example because it shows all of the true facts about money.

Which to me I have no formal education of.

Here are some things to consider as you begin becoming more comfortable with money and its side effects:

1) Quick money won't ever last - unless you make a plan to keep it.

2) Money with no plan will leave you worse off than you started.

3) Money that is not honest will haunt you forever.

4) Manage your money with a long term vision, instead of looking for short lived happiness.

5) When making financial decisions, look at the best bang for your buck as the barometer versus how much you can afford to spend.

   I wish I'd known this when I first started out.

   I spent one whole year living in a penthouse I was throwing half of my income at, when I could have been using that money as a down payment towards a rental property.

Especially in today's climate, when most of the people working are just thankful to have a job.

Comparing your behind the scenes with other peoples highlight reels is just plain stupid.

Use your money to pursue what genuinely makes you happy, and also helps build and secure your future.

The key to effective money management is to live within your means, and stay humble.

This is the breakdown I use to run my finances, which has helped me build the foundation for my future over the last few years:

1) The most obvious one is to spend less than you make.

Sounds simple, but without a clear budget is near impossible.

Living within your means seems like the most obvious thing to do, but so many people get lost and before you know it you are way overextended.

I love using Excel because of its simplicity, but any app or expense form will do.

Calculate your overhead expenses (How much it costs to live) and see where you can lean out.

That $35 box subscription adds up over the course of the year.

Remember: True long term wealth comes from repetitive actions and small, smart decisions of how you use your income.

2) Don't spend more than 30% of your income on Rent.
Some markets that might be hard to do.

If you find that you are struggling financially, now might be a good time to consider moving to an area that will better help you meet your financial goals.

3) Save a percentage of your income. In addition to having a rainy day fund, put aside as much as you can into a savings account that you will be able to use in your future.
30-50% is the sweet spot.

4) Invest in your education. Obviously I am not talking about traditional high schools and colleges. I am referring to self investing into things you want to learn more about.

Funny to me that I am the one saying this, but

honestly the more money I find myself spending on books, seminars, and mastermind groups has helped me cull the experiences from other people so I can learn from their mistakes and not have to make them on my own. More on that later.

In the famous words of Dr seuss:

" The more you read, the more you know. The more you know, the farther you will go. "

5) Insurance is one of those things you hope you never need, but it's great to have when you need it. You want to invest in a good plan that will help you should you ever need it.

For example, no one wants to get sick, but having a good health insurance plan helps ensure that your costs are more affordable.

The same goes for auto insurance, life insurance, and home insurance.

When you have a good plan, you're better able to handle life's unexpected situations.

6) Lastly, Invest in something that has a history of success and can be considered a sound investment.

STOCKS DO NOT COUNT

I advise my clients to always first consider real estate rentals in your area, for instance. Or Look to your local financial planner for more info and advice.

These are things I wish I would have known before I made my first money and applied it before it was too late and I had to start over.

I hope these are tips that will help you.

Chapter 33

After I went on to work for myself, the first few times I touched success I went and bought things to try and make me happy, and feel good.

Rightfully so.

Do not get me wrong, you are entitled to reward yourself AFTER you close a deal, or achieve a big goal.

Not only that but I strongly recommend it.

Giving yourself the opportunity to celebrate an achievement and take it all in is the best way to make sure wins stay constant.

How you choose to reward yourself however, should be strictly in line with your goals.

Once you commit to the self growth process **EVERYTHING** you do revolves around your goals.

When I first started out in my journey my only goal was to prove everyone wrong and become so successful I could do whatever I wanted.

I leased an expensive car.
I lived in an expensive house.

I used Drugs.
I went to expensive restaurants.
I bought expensive designer clothing.
I road tripped across America and traveled internationally.

Nothing was able to fill the void I was feeling.

Hard as I try.

Over the last few months I was moving so high paced and experiencing so many changes.

 Anything I was able to do in order to avoid facing the truth:

You are only as strong as you are honest, and honesty with myself was a very hard problem.

All this time I was using the new life I was living as a way to distract myself and suppress as much as I could from the real traumas I had from my past, and just focus on pushing forward.

Usually, that's the best way to go, but with trauma things just don't work like that.

I was trying Temporary Fixes for things that to me seemed permanent. Nothing seemed to be working.

My anger consumed my mind and prevented me from growing.

My sadness influenced my decisions in the hunt of temporary happiness.

My fear held me back from allowing myself to pursue new opportunities and connect with people authentically.

My pain from all the people who hurt me biting deep into my soul, I soon found myself on the path of an addict frantically trying to numb and calm my inner being.

This all led me down a very dark and dangerous path where I was my own enemy and kept doing loops of doom.

First began the waves of depression.
Then began the vicious spirals of anxiety.
Then the self doubt and loathing.

I started slipping into a downward spiral of abusing alcohol and watching pornography.

I drank to numb the haunting thoughts at night.
I watched porn to try and Unfuck My Feelings towards women and distract myself with the sad reality I was living in.

These were things I started doing more and more often to try and make my mind stop eating itself.

I drank myself stupid drunk in my brand new unfurnished penthouse apartment and proceeded to do the same thing over and over again for the following two weeks.

I convinced myself that I was doomed.

I was an alcoholic of sorts from the time I was 14 because I went to yeshivah where gross consumption of alcohol was not only not frowned upon, in some places it was even encouraged.

Pornography started consuming my mind, and alcohol numbed any feelings I had towards anything else.

As an alcoholic, you will violate your standards, quicker then you can lower them.

My anger consumed my mind and prevented me from growing.

My sadness influenced my decisions in the hunt of temporary happiness.

My fear held me back from allowing myself to pursue new opportunities and connect with people authentically.

My depression controlled my every decision and put me into a downward spiral I felt like I had no chance of getting out of.

My pain from all the people who hurt me biting deep into my soul, I soon found myself on the path of an addict frantically trying to numb and calm my inner Being.

This all led me down a very dark and dangerous path where I was my own enemy and kept doing loops of doom.

I was stuck and needed help.

I had to learn how to help myself.

I had the mindset of victimhood and doom.

I was unhappy, depressed, and sad.

I knew I deserved better.

I set out on the journey of a lifetime,

Just under 6 years ago I was torn between attempting to end my life again or investing in the unknown.

I chose life over death.

I chose opportunities over certainty.

I chose facts over my perceptions.

The fear was rampant.

The anxiety controlled me.

But the thought of waking up the next morning in the same spot made me shudder.

I did not know who I'd become.

I did not know who I'd meet.

I don't even know if I'd still have tomorrow what I have today.

I do know, however, that every day I wake up is a new opportunity.

Every day is a new day.

No matter the struggles of yesterday, or the history that precedes it, each and every day is an opportunity again to create a new reality.

YOUR reality.

6 years ago I wasn't connected to God, had no relationship with my parents, and in addition to my own self limiting beliefs - I actually believed that others' perception of me, in some sort of way defined me.

Today I am happy.

Today I am fulfilled.

Today I choose to embrace myself for who I am, and take advantage of all the gifts God has bestowed on me.

I have every reason to quit, yet I choose to carry on.

I choose to create my own reality.

I choose to follow my purpose.

I choose to do what makes me happy.

The truth is, that without the support of my friends and relationships I've built I wouldn't have stood a chance.

I am grateful for those who have impacted my life - both past, present, and future - and I'm looking forward to what tomorrow brings.

Sometimes you have to walk away in order to experience things on your own and be able to break free from anything that is holding you back from getting where you want to go.

There is nothing wrong with starting from the bottom and working your way up.

I did it.

There is nothing wrong with being broke and working your way to healthy credit.

I did it.

There is nothing wrong with being homeless and living with roommates.

I did it.

Matter of fact, most of the time you NEED a low in order to push you to greater heights.

I've been there.

I've learned that sometimes the lower you go, the higher you push to climb.

I've learned that sometimes you'll realize that what you've been running away from is really what you've needed.

I've learned that sometimes you'll end up in a completely different place than before.

I know that You owe it to yourself to find out.
It might just change your life.

Part four:

Building your dream life

I am going to spare you the gory details of my therapy and share with you a summary of the lessons I have spent Hundreds of hours and thousands of dollars on in the next chapters.

I am not a licensed therapist and if you are struggling with any sort of addictions or have any thoughts of intent of self harm, Please contact the National Suicide prevention line or call SAMHSA @

1-800-662-4357.

Chapter 34

It is no secret that pornography is frowned upon in today's society.

Over the past decade, there has been much debate about the merits and risks of viewing pornography.
Anti-porn advocates often argue that viewing erotic images can alter the brain and result in porn addiction. I want you to better understand what the data tells us about pornography, psychology, and the brain.

Both religiously and morally I believe it is wrong.

Pornography is addicting especially when the idea of sex is still novel and new to your mind.

Most kids I know came across it during puberty at the height of all the weird changes both in life and physically.

One of the biggest arguments for kids to be sheltered from the internet and technology is because one does not have to go very far to obtain pornography; there are literally millions of websites at an internet user's fingertips.

Matter of fact, estimates of the amount of internet use devoted to pornography range from 4% to 46% (of all internet use), according to the media.

Of course, they are worried.

Research on porn paints a more precise picture, including the following statistics:

- 46% of men and 16% of women between the ages of 18 and 39 intentionally view pornography in a given week.
- In a study of people ages 18-26, roughly two thirds (67%) of young men and one half (49%) of young women agree that viewing pornography is acceptable.
- In that same study, nearly 9 out of 10 (87%) young men and nearly one third (31%) of young women reported using pornography.
- Among the elderly, while sexual intercourse decreases, masturbation and the use of pornography increases.

Another interesting fact is that most people who use porn do not spend that much time on it. Some highlights, derived from the data collected through a survey conducted by the Kinsey Institute, reveal that:

- 66% of porn users view it for 5 hours or less a month.
- Another 16% of porn users view it for less than 15 hours a month.

- 6% use it for more than 26 hours a month and 3% use it for more than 50 hours per month.

One research study identified associations among pornography acceptance/use, emerging adults' risky sexual attitudes and behaviors, substance abuse patterns, and non-marital cohabitation values.

As humans, we are ingrained with the idea of procreation. I think this is one of the reasons people gravitate towards it.

I also remember the Stigma associated with sexual purity and piety where of which sex was never discussed, and was left to our imagination.

Even though porn addiction isn't widely accepted as an addiction, I can tell you from firsthand experience it will decimate your life if you let it.

For a short while, it literally took over my life.

I watched it a few times a day

- After a while - I wasn't just watching for pleasure I needed to watch it.
- I used it to comfort myself emotionally
- I felt guilty about it
- I would struggle to resist the urge and eventually succumb to it.

When I started talking about it in therapy I came to the realization that for me, porn was my outlet for reliving and reimagining the rape I experienced, and needed it in order to show my brain that what happened to me was not normal.

Having sex was me proving to myself that I am normal and able to function

I spent time digging deeper into it and found a way to overcome my addiction using unconventional therapy methods.

As porn use has become more widespread, the reasons for its use have diversified. **There are both benefits and risks associated with pornography.** The availability of porn has made it possible for a number of individuals who might have felt insecure or guilty about their sexuality, or sexual desires, to be able to gain familiarity and comfort with practices that are closer to their realm of experience. Some examples include:

- Monogamous couples seeking greater sexual satisfaction in their relationship.
- People living in remote areas, far from meaningful social networks.
- People who seek to satisfy fantasies in which their partners and spouses do not wish to engage; pornography provides a way to mitigate potential frustration while remaining committed to their relationship.

For some users, pornography provides a way to cope with the difficulties they might be facing, such as stress, depression, or loneliness. **Problems can ensue when use accompanies impulsivity, or when users do not feel they have control over their use.**

Recent research has shown that **non-drug addictions such as gambling, binge-eating, and sexual activities affect brain function in ways similar to alcohol and drug addiction.** Many addiction studies focus on what is referred to as the pleasure/reward circuitry and their corresponding neurotransmitters - chemicals that are responsible for the communication between neurons. One of the neurotransmitters frequently identified as central to addiction is dopamine. A behavior or drug that produces pleasure. It induces a rush of dopamine that ultimately "reinforces" that behavior, making it more likely to occur. The amygdala, basal ganglia, and other reward centers play a role in the reinforcement of the activity that produces pleasure.

Changes in the brain's neural pathways are referred to as "plasticity"; and "synaptic plasticity" refers to changes among neuronal connections

Research substantiates the idea that **porn addiction can alter brain plasticity. Non-drug addictions, like the internet and pornography use, may lead to changes similar to those reported with long-term drug use.** [14]

Additionally, increased pornography use is associated with:

- **Smaller volume and less activity in the striatum**- a region involved in processing rewards- although it is not yet clear if this is due to greater time spent viewing porn, or if people with reduced striatum volume will tend to watch more porn.
- These individuals also tend to have **less connectivity between the striatum and areas of the prefrontal cortex, indicating reduced judgment, decision making, or control over impulsive behaviors.**

Therapy might be a good place to start if you think you're having a problem with porn.

Your therapist will probably ask about your feelings surrounding porn, the function it serves, how often you use it, and how this use has affected your life.

You might also consider finding a local support group.

Ask your therapist or a doctor if they know of any sexual health support groups that focus on sex compulsions or out of control sexual behaviors in your area.

You could also look for online support groups if you can't find any local in-person meetups.

For a long time, I thought that I was watching porn because I was depressed.

The idea that using porn can trigger depression is widespread — but it isn't founded in any scientific research. There are no studies that show that using porn can cause depression.

Some research has shown that you're more likely to be depressed if you believe that you're "addicted" to porn.

If your usage is causing you distress, you may find it helpful to talk to a therapist or join a local support group.

Given all of the facts, if you watch porn regularly I strongly encourage you to stop.

Leave the religious guilt BS out of it - it will literally mess with your head.

That being said, below are my 10 steps to overcoming the urge to stop watching porn.

My life has become clearer since I've stopped.

Here is something I wrote 18 months after I stopped watching.

I've struggled with addiction.

I've struggled with depression.

I've struggled with finding satisfaction.

I used to feel helpless and overcome with anxiety and stress because of not knowing who I was.

I've watched hundreds of minutes of pornography.

I've spent many days in bed looking for a will to live.

I've done a lot of things in the name of finding happiness.

I've spent a lot of time hating myself.

I've spent a lot of time loving myself.

I've spent a lot of time not sure who I was.

Over time I learned to overcome my addiction.

Over time I learned how to deal with depression.

Over time I learned that contributing to others is a pillar of who I am.

I was stuck and needed help.

I had to learn how to help myself.

18 months ago I challenged myself to stop watching pornography and never look at it again.

I've proven myself I'm capable of anything I set my mind to.

547.5 days without any porn has allowed me to change who I've become and clear and open my head to experience and live the amazing reality of my life and be present in all of my relationships.

It has been an honor to serve the last 18 months in the IDF paratroopers brigade and sacrifice, grow, experience and learn so many amazing things about myself and the world around me.

I'm so humbled.

To all of my friends, family, and people who support me, thank you for being a part of my journey.

I'm grateful for having you in my life.

10 steps to overcome "The Urge" and stop using porn:

1) You must acknowledge that an addiction exists.
   The only way to be able to overcome anything you struggle with in life is to face it.

2) Understand that what you are doing is directly affecting your life and that of your partner. Even your future partners and relationships can be affected by it.
   Watching porn sets unrealistic expectations for yourself about sex and sexuality.

3) Get support.
   It is ok to reach out to others for help. I wish I had the support available today to work through this.

4) Identify your triggers.

For me, I saw patterns that I learned how to avoid and stop.

5) Find something to distract you when the urge comes.

I found things to reward myself with for resisting the urge when it set on.

6) Track your progress

I wrote myself a brag list and every time I broke the cycle I made a note of the date and time. Over time it became a lot easier

7) Start reading more about relationships and the steps to leading a healthy sex life.

There are some beautiful books on sexual health and wellness and I strongly encourage you to find something that matches your style.

8) Learn how to control your urges.

We live in an instant reward society. Everything needs to be "Here & Now". teach yourself abstinence by finding something that has positively affected you as you get better at it.

9) Give yourself the time needed to work through it.

We all mess up and sometimes our animalistic urges take over before we can control them. Take every mess up in stride and talk with an accountability partner and make a plan.

10) Take it one day as it comes.

As with any addiction, there are many loops and spirals your brain will put you through in order to get its fix. I believe you have the power to overcome any obstacle and achieve anything you set your mind to.

Chapter 35

Who you surround yourself with greatly determines who you are going to become.

There is a well known quote " Show me your friends, and I will show you the future".

That being said, you also need to make sure that when the universe puts these types of friends in your path, you are operating on a frequency that will communicate with them .

If you want to have high powered and successful friends, you must first work on yourself to be capable of handling and managing the power and success.

A healthy life will give you healthy foundations to build and grow on.

If those foundations aren't healthy then they will eventually disappear.

As a real estate agent I know how important a foundation report is when buying or selling a house; the home could be a gorgeous, million dollar mansion but the foundation could be rotting - which renders the house useless and to the point that it needs to be torn down.

I would very soon learn that a business is only as strong and reliable as its owner.

All this time I was using the life I was living as a distraction from the trauma and problems I had lived.

I was ignoring the feelings of depression and the affects anxiety and stress were taking a toll on my body.

It almost pushed me over the edge. More than once.

This is something I wrote that portrays how I felt and the radical change that affected me the second time I tried to end my life.

"I remember the day I wrote my suicide letter.//
Thinking about what I wanted to write was even harder than deciding what I wanted to do.//
It's so hard to talk when you want to kill yourself.//
Your thought process isn't the same as it usually is.//
I found myself struggling for words.//
Not the mental writers block trying to find words.//
It's a physical struggle.//
I just needed a rest.//
It just kept coming.//
People think that there is no fight involved.

They say suicidal people are weak or seeking attention.

They forget all the mental struggles faced because most of the time no one knows they are even going on.

Quite a few times in my life I experienced feelings maybe similar to what you are feeling right now, and all I wanted to do was escape it.

But they are a necessary part of life.

Once you're experiencing it all you need is endurance.

The natural change of emotions I am experiencing as I write this - as are you reading this - eventually kicks in for everyone.

The process takes time to kick in.

The truth is it gets hard and boring.

The trick is to find something to distract yourself just long enough to be able to change perspective.

I taught myself to use the distractions to create a life worth living where I control what takes up space in my life, and how I define happiness.

Then to use the pain as fuel to my journey.

I learn to not give a fuck about what anyone has to say about how I live my life and how to ask for help when I need it.

It goes without saying that I am glad I did not die on that day in 2014 but my pain was so real and raw I break into a sweat when I think about it.

I live my life today as a symbol of living proof that it is possible to live an active, healthy and productive life, filled with love and happiness even though I live with depression.

I wake up every morning and find a reason to hang on for just one more day.

Then make the day worth living.

I did that yesterday, and I will do that tomorrow.

I will do that every day for the rest of my life.

Just in case there are people watching me looking for a reason to hang on.

I'll be damned if I lose hope.

The sad fact is that there are alot of people I know who struggle with depression.

I live with Depression.

Lots of people struggle to understand what it means to be depressed.

Depression is living in a body that fights to survive, with a mind that tries to die.

Depression is like being colorblind, yet constantly being told how the world looks.

Depression is when sleep becomes an escape.

Depression is being afraid to be happy, because whenever you're happy something bad always happens.

Depression is sometimes wondering to yourself if death is better than life.

Depression is having so many thoughts and feelings, yet not having any words to share them.

Hold on to this hope: You can learn to manage your depression just like I did and live a happy fulfilling life.

The truth is that the damage life has inflicted on me in many places, has left me stronger and more resilient.

It's why I choose to say " I Battle" with depression Instead of "I Suffer" with it.

Because when depression hits, I hit back.

How to use your insecurities as fuel for growth ***

Insecurities short and simple are a lack of self confidence.

A lack of self confidence can come from experiences, mental health state, or simply misinformation.

The easiest way to stop these things from controlling you is to put a plan of action in place with clear steps to follow when you are feeling overwhelmed and foggy minded.

Self confidence is closely tied to depression and anxiety.

You're depressed because of how you feel about yourself, so you get anxious every time you have to do something where you feel people are judging you.

Truth is no one gives a fuck about you or anything you're doing, until you are making moves so big they can't ignore you.

I was this person.

Constantly scared of my own shadow, worrying about what other people were saying behind my back and c my feelings for other people's satisfaction.

The way I've been able to overcome all of these setbacks and grow into the person I've become is by getting extremely clear on what I want to become and what I'm willing to do to get there.

I made lists of do's and don'ts, of the triggers and how to deal with them.

The only way to come to a battle and win no matter what comes your way is to prepare for the unknown.

How you prepare is one hundred percent dependent on how truthful you are ready to be with yourself and how committed you actually are to a better life.

Things get better.

Things get worse.

Things will always get worse before they get better.

Most people don't stick around to see the full cycle.

Sometimes you need to step outside, get some air, regroup and remind yourself who you are and who you want to be.

And that's ok.

So long as you keep going.

One year ago today I started my journey in the Israel Defense Forces.

It's been a wild ride to say the least.

One things for sure, when shit hits the fan I keep fucking spinning.

Cheers to you and your personal growth journey.

Six years ago I never would have thought I would even be close to the person I am today.

At 18 years old,

✘ I was Angry.

✘ I was Sad.

✘ I was fearful.

✘ I was depressed.

✘ I was hurt.

My anger consumed my mind and prevented me from growing.

My sadness influenced my decisions in the hunt of temporary happiness.

My fear held me back from allowing myself to pursue new opportunities and connect with people authentically.

My depression controlled my every decision and put me into a downward spiral I felt like I had no chance of getting out of.

My pain from all the people who hurt me biting deep into my soul, I soon found myself on the path of an addict frantically trying to numb and calm my inner being.

This all led me down a very dark and dangerous path where I was my own enemy and kept doing loops of doom.

🚫 Turns out that when I cut out all of the negative influences in my life I was able to get a clear idea of who I wanted to become. 🚫

✅ I stopped swallowing what the media tried to ✅ feed me.

✅ I stopped hanging out with my shitty friends.

☑ I stopped trying to please everyone and did things that would make me happy.

‼ Turns out that when you cut out all of the negative influences it's possible to get a clear idea of who You want to become. ‼

Today I have the opportunity to create my own future and not one that is predetermined for me.

Today I am able to choose who I want to associate myself with and make sure that these people are aligned with my goals.

Today I am honored to have people in my life who value, appreciate and support me in chasing my goals and living my dreams.

From the bottom of my heart I want to thank you for supporting me and encouraging me to go out and do what I love.

Here are ten steps I use to keep my thoughts under control and my

1) know you are not alone. Seek out and find people you can feel comfortable with who will support you no matter what.

Lots of the battles that are going on inside in your head, it's a lot easier to carry when you have somebody to share it with. Reaching out to people who won't judge you will allow you to feel vulnerable and safe and will help you feel better yourself.

2) find ways to support and contribute to other people - even if you won't see immediate results.

The more I contribute to others, be it a phone conversation, a business consultation, or even just spend an hour listening, the more human I feel and more in touch with myself I get.

A candle loses nothing by lighting another candle.

In fact, it's quite the opposite.

Being selfishly selfless and sharing your talents with others is one of my favorite things to do.

3) Turn off your phone for at least one hour a day.

As an entrepreneur who's businesses are 85% cloud based, I am addicted to my phone.

The farthest it used to ever get away from me was my pocket.

These days I make time to just shut it down and get out to appreciate the world around me.

A walk on the beach, a walk in the park, a trip to the local dog shelter, a passion project.

Make a list of things you'd like to do and reference back to them when you are looking for something to do instead of binge watching Netflix.

Do things that you'll be able to look back on and be proud of.

Everything you do comes back around.

Be the captain of your own ship.

The first thing I had to internalize and understand when I was learning how to manage my depression and self doubt was that things can only control me if I give them the power to control me.

What that means plain and simple is that when I gave something meaning I gave it the power to affect me.

Be it for good.

Be it for bad.

For 80% of people, the first thing they see in the morning and the last thing they see at night is their phone.

This means that over 80% of Human beings today are being controlled by other peoples ("Influencers"") videos, views, opinions, and messages that were designed to have effects on your emotions and overall being.

This is a pander to your mind and slowly you relinquish control.

You cannot be in control of your life if you cannot even control the messages you see on your screen.

One of the best and most effective ways I've found to be able to almost always predict the outcome of any situation I found myself in was to be in control of the mindset I had while I was going into it, have a clear objective, and always fight to maintain my focus on what I wanted the outcome to be.

I set standards.

I got rid of my expectations.

I found my passion and focused on doing the things that make me feel good and fulfilled.

I made some rules with myself that I would stick to come hell or high water:

I will never give up.

I will never let frustration knock me down.

I will never let fear stand in my way.

I will never let time get into my head.

Time and time again I've had to remind myself that it does not matter how many tries it takes or how much time goes by.

It's OK to feel sorry for yourself and experience pain, but you have to accept the pain for what it is and allow yourself to process it and move on.

That does not mean that things now have the power to control you or dictate the pattern you are going to continue taking.

Emotional awareness and being mindful of how you choose to deal with each and every situation has a direct impact on your past, present and future.

Disappointment becomes obsolete when they aren't tied to any expectations.

Remember that.

Dealing with Stress and anxiety sucks.

Here is an acronym I came up with that has helped me navigate through the unchartered waters of anxiety that I still to use to this day:

Stop.

Think.

Regroup.

Execute.

Smile.

Surprise.

I strongly believe it is one of the reasons I have never been able to hold down a job working for someone else more than once.

A business owner is someone who has a vision more than what the average person sees, and works dedicatedly to bring it to life - regardless of what other people think or say.

Working a straight salary job never worked for me because I was always striving to grow, and the managers don't like that because they are worried I might become better than them.

When I set out to do things on my own I
there is a profound quote that goes like this: " Those who can, do. Those who can't; Teach.

I saw that really clearly how in the beginning when I let people know I was
set out to learn, then I was going to do it.

One day when I had my own team I was going to teach. When you set out into the world of opportunity remember these three things to make sure you do not end up like me:

The boy on the left is me four years ago.

The man on the right is me today.

Four years ago I made the decision to leave the religious world I grew up in and take my own path.
When I left, I had the mindset of victimhood and doom.
I was blessed to grow up in an amazing family with great parents, but deep down I was unhappy, depressed, and sad.
I knew I deserved better.
I set out on the journey of a lifetime, and although it's been hard and seems to never let up. Each day I push myself to leave it all out on the table and dial it up to the max.
Truth be told,
I'm not always motivated.

I'm not always feeling up to it.

I'm not always sure if I will see a return.

I am however, always refocusing my mindset and using my purpose to propel me forward in the pursuit of my dreams.

Four years ago I was torn between attempting to end my life again or investing in the unknown.

I chose life over death.

I chose opportunities over certainty.

I chose facts over my own perceptions.

The fear was rampant.

The anxiety controlled me.

But the thought of waking up the next morning in the same spot made me shudder.

I don't know who I'll become.

I don't know who I'll meet.

I don't even know if I'll still have tomorrow what I have today.

I do know, however, that every day I wake up is a new opportunity.

Every day is a new day.

No matter the struggles of yesterday, or the history that precedes it. Each and every day is an opportunity again to create a new reality.

YOUR reality.

Four years ago I wasn't connected to God, had no relationship with my parents, and in addition to my own self limiting beliefs - I actually believed that others' perception of me, in some sort of way defined me.

Today I am happy.

Today I am fulfilled.

Today I choose to embrace myself for who I am, and take advantage of all the gifts God has bestowed on me.

I have every reason to quit, yet I choose to carry on.

I choose to create my own reality.

I choose to follow my purpose.

I choose to do what makes me happy.

The truth is, that without the support of my friends and relationships I've built I wouldn't stand a chance.

I am grateful for those who have impacted my life - both past, present, and future - and I'm looking forward to what tomorrow brings.

Sometimes you have to walk away in order to experience things on your own and be able to break free from anything that is holding you back from getting where you want to go.

There is nothing wrong with starting from the bottom and working your way up.

There is nothing wrong with being broke and working your way to healthy credit.

There is nothing wrong with being homeless and living with roommates.

Matter of fact, most of the time you NEED a low in order to push you to greater heights.

Sometimes the lower you go, the higher you push to climb.

Sometimes you'll realize that what you've been running away from is really what you've needed.

Sometimes you'll end up in a completely different place than before.

You owe it to yourself to find out.

It might just change your life.

Made in the USA
Coppell, TX
21 December 2022

90369358R00215